Outlaw Tales
of Arizona

True Stories of Arizona's Most Famous
Robbers, Rustlers, and Bandits

Jan Cleere

TWODOT®

GUILFORD, CONNECTICUT
HELENA, MONTANA
AN IMPRINT OF THE GLOBE PEQUOT PRESS

A · **T W O D O T**® · **B O O K**

Copyright © 2006 Morris Book Publishing, LLC

Front cover photo: Pearl Hart holdup reenactment, Sharlot Hall Museum Photo, Prescott, Arizona. Back cover photos: Apache Kid and Albert Alvord courtesy of the Arizona Historical Society/Tucson.
Map by Multi-Mapping Ltd. © Morris Book Publishing, LLC

Library of Congress Cataloging-in-Publication Data
Cleere, Jan.
  Outlaw tales of Arizona : true stories of Arizona's most nefarious crooks, culprits, and cutthroats / Jan Cleere.—1st ed.
     p. cm.—(Outlaw tales series)
  Includes bibliographical references.
  ISBN-13: 978-0-7627-2814-5
  ISBN-10: 0-7627-2814-0
  1. Outlaws—Arizona—History—19th century. 2. Outlaws—Arizona—Biography. 3. Crime—Arizona—History—19th century.
  I. Title. II. Series.
  HV6452.A7C54 2006
  364.1092'2791—dc22

                                                                2005026029

Manufactured in the United States of America
First Edition/Second Printing

Outlaw Tales
of Arizona

To my husband Bob,
one of the good guys

Contents

Acknowledgments

I was fortunate to have the assistance and guidance of the following individuals, organizations, and institutions while researching *Outlaw Tales of Arizona*. We all share a love of history and a desire to bring the stories of Arizona's past to future generations.

Arizona is graced with a profusion of historians and writers who willingly volunteer their knowledge and expertise. Tucson's Arizona Historical Society Historian Jim Turner never failed to answer my often obscure questions. His knowledge of Arizona history is truly amazing. Thanks to Mesa Community College historian and instructor Paul T. Hietter; Arizona State Library, Archives and Public Records Archivist Nancy Sawyer; and authors Phyllis de la Garza and Wynne Brown for their learned assistance.

I am grateful to the library and research staffs at the Arizona Historical Society in Tucson, the Special Collections Divisions of the University of Arizona in Tucson and Northern Arizona University in Flagstaff, and the research staff at the Sharlot Hall Museum in Prescott. Their collections are invaluable to any researcher.

Smaller historical societies across Arizona contain fascinating, sometimes unexplored, accounts of our more notorious citizens. I am indebted to H. Christine Reid at the Pinal County Historical Society Museum in Florence, Lynn and Bill Haak at the Gila County Historical Museum in Globe, and Ann Garlinghouse at the Gila County Courthouse.

My editor Stephanie Hester, who has been a staunch supporter of my work, deserves special recognition for her expertise, guidance, and kindhearted spirit.

To my family and friends, thanks for keeping me sane when one of these dang desperadoes frustrated me to the brink that I considered hanging every one of them all over again.

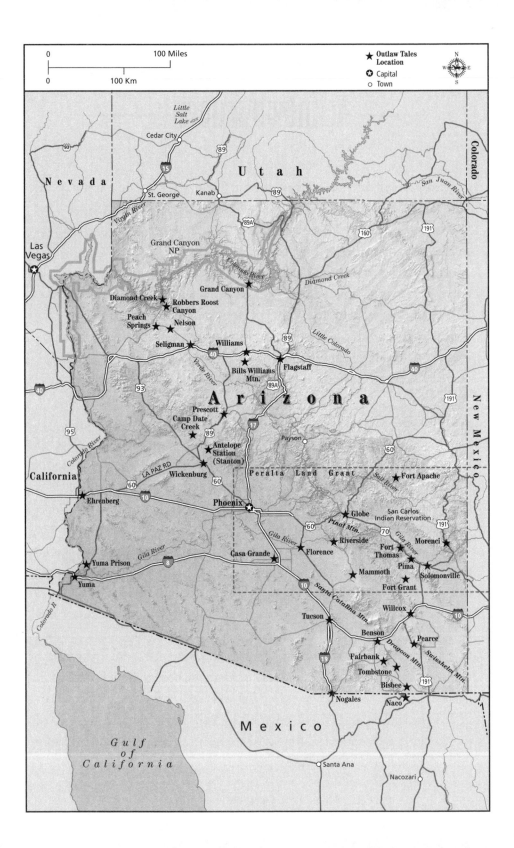

0   100 Miles
0   100 Km

N
W E
S

Nevada

Little Salt Lake

Cedar City

Utah

89

15

St. George

Kanab

89

Colorado

San Juan River

Las Vegas

Virgin River

89A

160

191

Grand Canyon NP

Colorado River

Diamond Creek

Grand Canyon ★

Diamond Creek ★

★ Robbers Roost Canyon

Peach Springs ★

★ Nelson

Little Colorado

Seligman ★

Williams ★

40

89

Flagstaff ★

40

A r i z o n a

Bills Williams Mtn. ★

89A

191

93

Verde River

Prescott ★
Camp Date Creek ★

89

17

Payson ○

60

N e w   M e x i c o

★ Antelope Station (Stanton)

Wickenburg ○

60

Peralta Land Grant

Salt River

★ Fort Apache

LA PAZ RD

California

Colorado River

95

Ehrenberg ★

60

10

Phoenix ✪

Globe ★

San Carlos Indian Reservation

70

60

Pinal Mtn.

★ Riverside

Fort Thomas ★

Gila River

Morenci ★

191

Casa Grande ★

Florence ★

Gila River

Pima ★

★ Solomonville

Yuma Prison ★

8

Gila River

Yuma ★

★ Mammoth

Fort Grant ★

10

Colorado R.

Santa Catalina Mtn.

Willcox ★

10

Tucson ★

Benson ★

Dragoon Mtn.

Pearce ★

19

Fairbank ★

Swisshelm Mtn.

191

Tombstone ★

Bisbee ★

191

Nogales ★

Naco ★

M e x i c o

Gulf
of
California

Santa Ana ○

Nacozari ○

——Introduction——

Uncovering the true history of an outlaw is like trying to tame a rattlesnake. Just when you think you have mastered the complete story of one of these desperadoes, some new piece of evidence surfaces that poisons your theories to the bone.

Contradictions abound for those researching the lives and legends of elusive lawbreakers. It's these unsolved mysteries that keep historians and writers sequestered in dusty, spider-webbed archives thumbing with ink-stained fingers through crumbling newspapers and ancient parchments, searching for that elusive, as yet undiscovered document that will make their work more true and compelling than all previously written. Sometimes, I suspect these long-ago outlaws are sitting around their campfires in Hell laughing at those of us trying to make sense of the legacies they left behind.

Arizona claims its share of these varmints whose lives are complicated by myth, mystique, and a goodly dose of mayhem. In fact the abundance of crooks roaming through Arizona Territory in the rough and often violent 1800s was one of the factors that kept statehood at bay until 1912. Their misdeeds ran the gamut from train and stagecoach robbery to horse and cattle rustling to murder, larceny, and fraud. They came from across the nation looking for gold, silver, copper, and unsuspecting, naive individuals to rob, swindle, and slay.

Outlaws were so prevalent in Arizona Territory that in 1877 Governor Anson Peacely-Killen Safford ranted they "are a scourge to civilization, a disgrace to humanity, and should be swept from the face of the earth as remorsely as the most ferocious wild beast." Five years later, the *Tombstone Epitaph*, still searching for a way to rid Arizona, and particularly the town of Tombstone, of its criminal element suggested "make[ing] it incumbent upon, not only officials, but all good citizens as well, to take such positive measures as will speedily rid this section of that murderous, thieving element which has made us a reproach before the world, and so seriously retarded the industry and progress of our country."

While Governor Safford was still in office (1869–1877), construction began in 1875 on Yuma Territorial Prison to house Arizona's numerous lawbreakers. More than 3,000 prisoners, including twenty-nine women, were incarcerated in the adobe and stone structure until it was replaced in 1909 by a new prison in Florence. Only twenty-six managed to escape from Yuma, although 140 tried.

But even while these miscreants were serving time or swinging from the end of a rope or dying from a dozen bullets plugged through their evil hearts, we were intrigued by their stories and devoured every word we heard and read. At times one story contradicted another, but we continued to amass these tales and often passed them along as truths. We relished hearing about the lawman gone bad and the outlaw with the heart of gold.

Today we continue to search for a substantiated fact or an ancient document that will prove the yarn told to us by a crusty old miner or sun-crazed cowboy. And maybe we will eventually unearth more facts about these outlaw men and women and toss aside the legends and mythology that have kept us spellbound for more than one hundred years. But sometimes I wonder if we will enjoy the truth as much as the fiction. Mystery and history go hand in hand, and Arizona history contains some of the best whodunits around.

The murderers and scoundrels presented in these pages come from all across the inhospitable wilderness territory, perpetrating their crimes on innocent pioneers attempting to settle an unforgiving land. Not everything about them can be proved beyond a reasonable doubt, leaving the reader's imagination to decide how much to believe and what should remain as just a good tale.

The Wickenburg
——⇒▸•◂—— Massacre ——⇒▸•◂——
Last Ride Out of Town

J ust after sunup on November 5, 1871, the Arizona Stage Company
coach, crowded with eight passengers, pulled out of Wickenburg for
its run to the Colorado River town of Ehrenberg, a distance of just
over 100 miles. All but one individual had started the journey the evening
before in Prescott. Aaron Barnett first boarded in Wickenburg and settled
in beside his sleepy riding companions. Just a few miles outside of
Wickenburg, he realized he had forgotten some unfinished business in
town. Asking the driver to stop, Barnett got off and watched as the carriage again headed west toward Ehrenberg before he set out on foot the
few short miles back to Wickenburg. Whatever Barnett forgot to do that
day saved his life. Of the remaining seven passengers and one driver on
the ill-fated stage, six would never live to see the sun rise again.

"Dutch" John Lance had been employed by the Arizona Stage
Company just a few weeks when he took the reins of the four-horse
coach early that Monday morning. This would be only his second trip
down the well-traveled La Paz Road from Wickenburg to Ehrenberg.
There were always reports of Indians waylaying travelers and even some
instances of murder along the central Arizona route, but he had no intention of letting his passengers fall to such a fate before he deposited them
in Ehrenberg. From there most would board a steamer for the run down-
river to Yuma and on to California. As he inspected the wagon one last
time, he watched his travelers climb aboard. They had enjoyed but a few
hours rest after arriving from Prescott well after midnight.

Peter Hamel and George Salmon climbed inside the coach, glad to be returning to their families in California after working with the Wheeler expedition, one of four research missions exploring western territories. The results brought back by these parties would include topographic and geologic maps, inventory of flora, fauna, strata, and mineral resources, plus interpretations of geologic occurrences. George M. Wheeler's survey was the only military expedition and had concentrated on water and terrain, studies that would affect future military operations.

Twenty-two-year-old journalist Frederick Wadsworth Loring had also traveled with the Wheeler expedition, reporting back to eastern publications. Before he left on the tour, Loring trimmed his hair very short and jokingly remarked that the Apaches would not find him a worthy adversary with so few locks to scalp. He chose to ride next to the driver.

Climbing up beside Loring and Lance, Charles S. Adams, who had been working in the flour depot of W. Bichard & Co. in Prescott, was grateful to be heading home to his wife and children in San Francisco.

Frederick Shoholm settled inside the coach beside Hamel and Salmon. Shoholm had recently sold his jewelry business in Prescott and was on his way to Philadelphia. He planned to board a ship in San Francisco and travel by way of Panama.

The only woman on the stage, twenty-four-year-old Mollie Sheppard, also had sold her business in Prescott and was reportedly carrying as much as $15,000 in cash, plus a large stash of jewelry. Mollie had run a successful house of pleasure since 1868, but it was time to get out of town and start elsewhere. She planned on settling in Panama City.

William Kruger, a clerk with Arizona Territory's Army Quartermaster, would leave the stage in Ehrenberg where he had business to conduct. He was supposedly carrying between $30,000 and $40,000 in military funds. Kruger's blemished reputation included a suspicion that he sometimes made a tidy profit from the sale of army mules and equipment.

Monument dedicated to the victims of the Wickenburg Massacre.
Arizona State Library, Archives and Public Records, Archives Division, Phoenix #95-9803

Once Aaron Barnett left the stage to walk back to Wickenburg, the remaining passengers started a card game of Freeze-Out, a popular gambling pastime. Mollie graciously spread her luxurious fur cape across everyone's knees to serve as a table. As was often the case, most of the passengers placed their weapons under the seat cushions so they could enjoy a more comfortable ride.

The stagecoach clipped along for the next hour without a hitch. About 8 miles out of Wickenburg, Dutch Lance had just started the horses into a wash when he saw the spindly bushes beside the road come to life. "Apaches!" he shouted as a band of marauders quickly surrounded the carriage, firearms blazing a torrent of bullets. The first salvo hit Lance dead on. As he dropped the reins, the horses careened off the road.

Inside the coach, Shoholm died with cards still in his hand, and Hamel fell across Mollie's fur coat. Within seconds another round of gunfire ratcheted across the wagon. Bullets slammed into Adams's spine, leaving him paralyzed and at the mercy of his assailants. Loring fell with a knife imbedded in his chest. Although Salmon managed to flee the coach, he was brought down within minutes.

Kruger, suffering only minor wounds, later claimed he threw the hysterical and wounded Mollie to the floor of the wagon to protect her from further gunfire. When the shooting abruptly ceased after just two volleys and a deadly calm enveloped the bloody wagon, Kruger waited only seconds before shoving Mollie out of the stage into the desert.

According to Kruger's later testimony, several gunmen chased the fleeing couple, but he managed to fight them off, even wounding two with his deadly aim, all the while keeping the fainting Mollie tucked under his arm. But one report credits Mollie with doing her share by threatening the approaching desperadoes with a broken whiskey bottle.

Kruger claimed the assailants pursued Mollie and him but a short distance before they scattered across the desert like a herd of cattle on the run.

The couple struggled along the desolate road until they spotted a mail wagon coming their way. The driver was horrified at the tale he heard, and, seeing Mollie's festering injuries—three bullet wounds plus wooden splinters from the coach deeply embedded in her arm—he sequestered the pair behind his wagon, gave them an ample supply of water, and rode off on a spare horse toward Wickenburg to report the ghastly killings. Kruger and Mollie were taken to Camp Date Creek for medical treatment with Mollie still clinging to her precious fur cape, its plush elegance riddled with nine bullet holes.

The dead were returned to Wickenburg for burial. Only Salmon was buried at the site and his body was eventually exhumed and interred beside the others. When *The Arizona Miner* reported the incident, it noted Salmon ". . . received a severe wound and fell from the stage, but recovering ran about twenty yards, was followed, overtaken, killed and scalped, the whole hair, ears, skin of the face being taken off to the mouth."

"Six men," said the *Miner*, "who . . . left Wickenburg full of life and hope and in the happy anticipation of soon again greeting their friends' after a prolonged absence—lay side by side, rigid in death and drenched in blood—the unavenged victims of a murder as dark and as damnable as ever stained the hands of an assassin."

Kruger and Mollie survived their injuries and eventually made it to California. But a few years later, Kruger reported that Mollie had succumbed to her wounds. She never made it to Panama City.

As the sole survivor, William Kruger often related his version of the Wickenburg Massacre, and many believed every word he said. Others, to this day, question many of his details of the slaying. There are almost as many opinions of who attacked the Wickenburg stagecoach that crisp November morning as there were victims of the massacre and mayhem.

Initial reaction placed blame on the Apache-Mohave (Yavapai) Indians sequestered at Camp Date Creek, about 25 miles from Wickenburg. Ironically, the camp was established to protect travelers along the La Paz Road. The attacking warriors, who were horseless, were purportedly wearing moccasins specific to the Apache-Mohave. The tribe formed its moccasins by pulling the upper part of its leather footgear down over the lower section and lacing it to the sole with rawhide, creating a distinct foot pattern. Other tribes in the area pulled the leather up around the top of the foot, leaving a smoother footprint.

The posse followed a trail that led to Camp Date Creek. Along the way they discovered a hunting bag containing bone powder, a sacred medicine among the Apache-Mohave. They also found a deck of cards with the corners cut off, a practice of local Indians. One of the most bizarre pieces of evidence investigated was excrement found at the massacre site that supposedly contained mesquite beans, a favorite of Indians in the area. Upon further investigation, however, the beans were found to be pumpkin seeds, which Indians rarely ate.

Within days of the massacre, several Apache-Mohave showed up with cash in their pockets and were immediately suspected of participating in the massacre. However, the Wells, Fargo box left at the murder scene, purportedly containing a great deal of cash, had not been opened.

Two men were scalped—Salmon and Hamel—and this almost solid-ified the argument that Indians had instigated the Wickenburg Massacre.

Enough evidence existed, however, to question whether Indians per-petrated the attack. Indians would not have left surviving horses (the lead horse had been killed and another wounded), as horse meat was a favorite dish. Colorful shawls, jewelry, and even the horses' leather har-ness would have been confiscated if Indians had been the culprits since these were all highly valued items. The surviving horses had been freed and the harness found neatly stacked. Indians would not have wasted time on this task.

Some of the mailbags were cut open, but the envelopes found strewn across the desert had been carefully torn off at one end, not ripped apart. Ammunition was left at the scene. Indians desperately needed ammunition and would not have ignored this stash.

The posse found no other tracks along the path traveled by William Kruger and Mollie Sheppard. If Indians had followed them, the couple would not have escaped—warring Indians rarely left survivors.

Kruger and Mollie both claimed they saw about fifteen men clad in blue soldier's trousers, standard issue for reservation Indians, coming at them with pistols blazing, but neither could positively say whether they were Indians, Mexicans, or white men.

Another faction held local white men responsible for purposely pointing the finger of blame at the Indians. Businessmen made money when native tribes rebelled as this forced the federal government to pump more money and troops into the territory.

Yet another conjecture blamed Mexican bandits for the attack, led by the nefarious outlaw Joaquin Barbe. About two months before the mas-sacre, a Mexican woman living in Wickenburg claimed she overheard a conversation between two Mexican men plotting a stage robbery. She warned her friends not to take the Wickenburg stage for the next few months.

In 1916 a dying man said he still carried a silver watch fob bearing the letter "L" that he had obtained from a Mexican woman in Wickenburg about three months after the robbery. He claimed the watch fob belonged to the reporter Frank Loring.

Mollie Sheppard believed a group of white men from Prescott, who had shown a keen interest in how much money she was carrying, might be responsible for the slaughter.

Since only the bags of Mollie and Kruger were broken into, a small group even suspected the couple may have perpetrated the biggest hoax by killing the passengers, then burying all the money they could carry in the desert, inflicting wounds upon themselves, and walking away from the ordeal much richer. Kruger claimed the attackers got away with close to $25,000.

Inspection of Kruger's gun when he arrived at Camp Date Creek showed it had not been fired even though he swore he had shot two of the attackers.

Debate still lingers over who laid in ambush for the Wickenburg stage as it bounced along the La Paz Road that cool November morning. Did the perpetrators kill for money, for revenge, or maybe just for sport? We may never know.

Journalist Fred Loring wrote of his experiences with the Wheeler expedition shortly before boarding the Wickenburg stage that fateful day. "I am bootless, coatless, everything but lifeless," he said. "I have had a fortnight of horrors. This morning an Indian fight capped the climax. However, I am well and cheerful." He had no idea what was in store for him.

Frank Nashville
"Buckskin Frank" Leslie
The Lady Killer

May Leslie's knees buckled as she awaited the next volley of gunfire. The slightest movement from her might be her last, and she commanded her body to remain as rigid as a rotting corpse as bullets whizzed about her head. Maybe one more round would satisfy the gunman. She heard the bullets click into the chamber as her husband prepared to fire again. He always took careful aim, as careful as anyone full of liquor could muster.

May watched him sway as he pointed the gun at her head. He slowly pulled the trigger and painted her portrait in bullets along the wall. As the gun clattered to the ground, so did Frank Leslie in a drunken stupor. May, known around Tombstone, Arizona, as the "Silhouette Girl" because of her husband's proclivity for shooting around her profile, fell in a trembling heap. She had survived seven years of marriage to Frank Leslie, a man of sweet charm and deadly aim, but she figured her odds of surviving one more year were not good.

Frank Leslie had been hanging around Tombstone since 1880, and he had earned a reputation as a hard drinking, free-fisted, fast-shooting, story-telling lady's man. He related so many versions of his origins that even he probably didn't remember the truth. He usually claimed he was born in the early 1840s in Texas, but once told a reporter his family roots were in Virginia. He also said he served in the Confederate Army as a bugler; studied medicine in Heidelberg, Germany; served as a deputy sheriff in Kansas under Wild Bill Hickok; prospected in

Frank Nashville "Buckskin Frank" Leslie, photo circa 1893.

Arizona State Library, Archives and Public Records, Archives Division, Phoenix #97-7081

Colorado; had been a roughrider in Australia and a boat pilot in the Fiji Islands; owned a bar in San Francisco; and served as an army scout in the Dakotas, Oklahoma, Texas, and along Arizona's borders. Somewhere he acquired the nickname "Buckskin Frank" and dressed to suit the title in a fringed buckskin jacket.

Of course Leslie never offered any proof of his past whereabouts or his accomplishments. Texas and Virginia birth records do not exist for Frank Nashville Leslie. Neither are there records of him serving in the Confederate Army, of him attending a Heidelberg medical school, or of any lawman named Leslie riding with Hickok.

A couple of his stories have a semblance of truth, however. He probably did serve as a scout on the San Carlos Indian Reservation around 1877. And he tended bar in a couple of saloons in San Francisco until he moseyed into Tombstone.

Tombstone in 1880 was a town filled with gambling dens, saloons, and houses of pleasure. Leslie found work bartending at the Cosmopolitan Hotel, a two-story wooden building boasting a veranda, ladies' parlor, and sitting rooms. The saloon advertised a variety of wines, liquors, "and the finest brands of cigars." When not working behind the bar, Leslie could be found visiting any number of Tombstone saloons imbibing enough liquor to satisfy an entire herd of trail-dry cattle. His proclivity for liquor was only surpassed by his eye for the ladies, and he dressed to please them in his buckskin jacket, custom-made boots, and pearl-studded shirts.

May Killeen had recently separated from her husband, Mike, and taken a room at the Cosmopolitan. She and Leslie had exchanged pleasantries on more than one occasion. On the night of June 22, 1880, May asked Leslie to escort her home from a dance, and Leslie was more than happy to oblige. They headed for the hotel accompanied by Leslie's friend, George Perine. No one noticed the shadowy figure watching as they entered the hotel.

Now Mike Killeen had already warned Leslie to stay away from his wife, and Leslie had taken the precaution of borrowing a gun for the evening. It was against the law to carry weapons in Tombstone; all had to surrender firearms at the first saloon they encountered upon entering town. But those who felt the need of protection could always borrow a gun from behind the bar. Leslie had no problem obtaining a weapon for his evening stroll with May Killeen.

Mike Killeen watched the threesome enter the hotel and wasted no time following his wayward wife and Frank Leslie. George Perine headed for the bar while Leslie and May made their way to the second-floor veranda. From his place at the bar Perine spied Killeen entering the hotel. He shouted to Leslie that Killeen was on his way with murder in his eye and a gun in his hand.

The roar of gunfire sent hotel guests stumbling sleepily from their rooms only to hastily retreat behind locked doors as the two men emptied their guns. Killeen tumbled down the stairs and into the saloon with Leslie in hot pursuit. From behind the bar, Leslie grabbed a second pistol and fired another round at Killeen. When the smoke cleared, Killeen lay mortally wounded. He lingered for six days, long enough to swear Leslie started the ruckus. Leslie insisted Killeen came in shooting and he had no recourse but to return fire.

Arrested and charged with Mike Killeen's murder, Leslie relied on his own testimony and that of the not-so-grieving widow to swear Killeen came onto the veranda with gun blazing. It didn't take the coroner's jury long to acquit Leslie on the grounds of self-defense.

On August 5, just weeks after Leslie was released from jail, the same judge who officiated at Leslie's court hearing pronounced Frank Leslie and May Killeen man and wife. The ceremony took place in the parlor of the Cosmopolitan Hotel. The *Tombstone Epitaph* congratulated the couple on their nuptials, lauding Leslie as *"un chavalier sans peur et sans reproche"* (a knight without fear and reproach).

Leslie moved down the street to the Oriental Saloon to work for owner Milt Joyce. The Earp brothers hung out at the Oriental and Leslie was welcome to drink with them, but he took no part in the infamous October 26, 1881, shootout at the O.K. Corral. Wyatt always said Leslie had the second fastest draw in the territory, just behind Doc Holliday.

Over the years Leslie developed an interest in prospecting and filed several mining claims in the Dragoon and Swisshelm Mountains. But he preferred life in town where drinking, gambling, and a little "bird" watching embodied his nightly pleasures. When he had money, he spent it. When he didn't get what he wanted, he turned surly and dangerous. Those were the nights May Leslie soon learned to dread. As old-time Tombstone resident Billy King noted, "He was a likable damn fellow when he was sober . . . but when he was tanked up he turned as sour as a barrel of Dago red."

Leslie's quick draw earned him a reputation on both sides of the badge. In March 1881, a detachment of eight lawmen set out from Tombstone on the trail of bandits who had held up the stagecoach as it headed toward Benson. The posse consisted of lawmen Wyatt, Vigil, and Morgan Earp; Cochise County Sheriff Johnny Behan and Deputy Sheriff Billy Breakenridge; and sworn-in deputies Doc Holliday, Bat Masterson, and Frank Leslie. Separating as they traveled, Leslie came upon one of the outlaws and reportedly sat down to eat with him before returning alone to Tombstone claiming he had lost the trail. Rumors circulated that Sheriff Behan, supposedly a friend of the robbers, had paid Leslie to ride a cold course.

The sun had barely risen above the horizon when Leslie walked into the Oriental Saloon on November 14, 1882, but already a group of men hovered near the bar having their usual liquored breakfast. Leslie was welcomed into their discussion, which may have had political overtones, and the men finished several rounds before cocky young Billy Claiborne entered the saloon about 7:30 A.M. Claiborne was as mean as an angry snake. He had ridden with the murdering cattle rustler John Ringo and often worked both sides of the border stealing cattle and horses. Claiborne blamed Leslie for John Ringo's death; Leslie and Ringo had been seen together shortly before Ringo was found straddling a tree with a bullet in his head.

It was obvious Claiborne had downed his breakfast at a neighboring watering hole. He sidled up to the group at the bar and immediately interrupted the conversation. Leslie took him aside and asked him to leave. But Claiborne refused and again butted into the assemblage. Leslie booted Claiborne out the saloon door. Claiborne shouted he would return to get even, but Leslie just turned his back on the youngster.

When Claiborne reappeared, he was carrying his Winchester. The street emptied as he headed toward the Oriental. "I don't allow any man to spit on me," he swore.

Leslie, warned that Claiborne was looking for him, left the saloon by a side door. Rounding the corner to the main street, he saw Claiborne hiding behind a fruit stand and warned the youngster not to shoot. But Claiborne stood up and fired, the bullet landing harmlessly at Leslie's feet. Leslie floored him with one shot. "I told him I was sorry," Leslie later stated. "I might have done more, but I couldn't do less."

Leslie again faced a coroner's jury pleading self-defense. He walked out of the courtroom a free man.

Milt Joyce, proprietor of the Oriental Saloon, also owned the Magnolia Ranch in the Swisshelm Mountains east of Tombstone. Leslie had a one-quarter interest in the place and Joyce left most of the ranching business in Leslie's hands. Since Leslie spent more time there than Joyce, the Magnolia was often mistakenly called Leslie's ranch.

In 1883 Leslie experienced a run-in with Apache raiders at the Magnolia. He lost most of the horses and about fifty head of cattle to the marauders. Two years later, in May 1885, when Geronimo and a band of Apaches escaped from the San Carlos Indian Reservation, Leslie was more than happy to hire on as a scout under Captain Wirt Davis. It took three months of hard riding before Davis and his men located Geronimo's camp. And although Geronimo escaped, the soldiers killed a handful of his men and captured a few women and children.

Davis sent Leslie to inform General George Crook of the battle. According to Leslie, he had to swim the Bavispe River eleven times in one day to deliver the report. Leslie knew how to make himself look good in the eyes of the law.

Each time Leslie returned from scouting, battling Apaches, and even one stint as an inspector along the Arizona-Sonora border looking for smugglers, he made up for lost time in the Tombstone saloons. He would then go home to May, slap her around a bit, and stand her up against the wall to practice his shooting. May knew she would soon die beneath his hands or at the end of his gun. On May 27, 1887, she filed for divorce, claiming Leslie beat and choked her along with framing her silhouette in bullets. She also accused him of infidelity. The court awarded May half of Leslie's interest in the Magnolia Ranch, which she immediately sold back to Milt Joyce. Leslie eventually sold Joyce his remaining interest, but continued to manage the place.

Leslie was soon seen dallying with Mollie Williams, also known as Mollie Bradshaw, Mollie Edwards, and Blonde Mollie, a singer at the Bird Cage Theater. She had arrived in town with a man named Mike Bradshaw. Shortly after Leslie made Mollie's acquaintance, Bradshaw lay dead with his head bashed in. Fingers pointed at Leslie, but no evidence was found implicating him. He and Mollie headed off into the Swisshelms, to Magnolia Ranch.

Unfortunately, they didn't stay put on the ranch and often spent days frequenting drinking establishments from one end of Tombstone to the other. Mollie could hold her own with Leslie and the two often loudly disagreed well into the night as they guzzled copious amounts of liquor.

In early July 1889, the couple headed into Tombstone to celebrate Independence Day. Their revelry continued for almost a week. Finally, hitching up their horses, they headed out of town, drunk when they left and still sotted when they arrived back at the ranch on July 10. An argument started in Tombstone continued to rage.

The next day, Leslie, still swilling a potent brew, rode over to William Reynolds's ranch where he informed his neighbor he was going to kill him. He ordered Reynolds to defend himself, but when Reynolds, who had obviously seen Leslie in this condition before, refused to pick up a rifle, Leslie left in a huff and staggered home.

James Neal worked off and on for Leslie at the Magnolia Ranch. He understood his boss's frequent fits of rage and usually stayed out of sight when trouble boiled. But on the night of July 11, he took pity on the tipsy Mollie and sat with her while Leslie was off harassing his neighbor. When Leslie returned, he suspected Neal and Mollie had been up to no good. After smacking Mollie around a few times, he determined he would "put a stop to all this." He picked up his pistol and aimed. With one shot, Mollie fell dead to the floor in a heap of skirts and petticoats.

Neal had no time to react before Leslie fired at him. "Don't be afraid, it's nothing," Leslie told him and, at first, Neal believed him. But as blood started trailing down his legs, Neal bolted through the door and into the desert. The next day, rancher Reynolds found him collapsed on his doorstep.

Leslie came looking for Neal at the Reynolds ranch and related the evening's events, claiming Neal had killed Mollie and he had shot Neal in self-defense. Reynolds denied seeing Neal, so Leslie assumed the young man lay dead somewhere in the desert and figured there would be no witnesses to dispute his story.

After Leslie left, Reynolds sent for the doctor who patched up Neal and took him into town. Neal told his story to the sheriff leaving little doubt who had perpetrated the double shooting.

Two days later, deputies found a disheveled Leslie riding along the road into town and took him to the sheriff. Distraught, Leslie confessed to killing Neal after Neal had slain his beloved Mollie. Suddenly, Neal appeared in the doorway, weak but strong enough to call Leslie a liar.

This time the jury did not agree with Leslie's self-defense argument. He was sentenced to serve the remainder of his life in the Yuma Territorial Prison for the murder of Blonde Mollie.

Leslie and ten other prisoners were escorted from the Cochise County Jail to Yuma Territorial Prison in January 1890 under the watchful eye of Sheriff John Slaughter. According to the *Tucson Citizen*, they all arrived drunk. Maybe Leslie was able to persuade the sheriff to make one last stop before sending him into the depths of Hell.

Leslie actually spent only seven years in Yuma Prison. There was talk he was part of an attempted breakout in March 1890, but no mention of the incident appears in prison records. For the most part, he was a model prisoner and spent most of his time working in the prison infirmary as a pharmacist.

In 1893 a reporter from the *San Francisco Chronicle* visited Leslie at the prison. He must have believed every word out of Leslie's mouth as the story he wrote is comprised of tall tales right from Leslie's vivid imagination. But when Belle Stowell of San Francisco read the *Chronicle* story, she began corresponding with Leslie and sending gifts of food and clothing to the imprisoned man. Eventually their friendship blossomed into love.

Leslie's exemplary behavior behind bars, plus the pleas of Belle Stowell and other friends who petitioned Arizona Territorial Governor Benjamin Franklin for his release, set him free on November 17, 1896. He ran right into the arms of Belle Stowell and the two were married in Stockton, California, on December 1.

How long the marriage lasted is uncertain, as Belle soon disappeared from Leslie's life. He went to Mexico in early 1897 to assist a geologist seeking coal deposits for the Southern Pacific Railroad. While there, he supposedly killed three men when they attempted to steal wood from the work site.

Leslie may have headed next for the Alaskan goldfields, but by 1902, he was back in San Francisco. When the *Chronicle* reported he sustained a gunshot wound as his pistol fell out of his pocket and went off, he told the reporter, "I suppose that my friends will tell me I'm not fit to carry a pistol. After forty years on the frontier to be hurt by my own gun, looks like it."

Leslie worked as a stocker for a couple of grocery stores and as a janitor in a billiard hall, but he usually lived off handouts from the barrooms he frequented. Wyatt Earp, now living in California, sometimes staked his old friend to a set of clean clothes and maybe a drink or two.

Leslie was last seen alive around 1920, sweeping floors in a San Francisco saloon. One night he disappeared, supposedly taking the bartender's gun with him. Maybe he was just borrowing it like he used to do in Tombstone. About three years later, a skeleton and rusty gun were found in the hills north of Martinez, California. The serial number on the gun was the same as the one taken from the bar that night. "If it [the story] is indeed real," said writer/historian Douglas Martin, "then Leslie was not all bad; he did one good thing before he died. He killed himself."

Leslie once admitted to killing thirteen men. "It was my fourteenth that caused all my trouble," he bemoaned. "But then, my fourteenth was a woman."

The Grime/Hawley Heist
A Tale from the Hanging Tree

I don't want to die with my boots on!" cried Lafayette Grime as he squatted on the dust-encrusted ground and took off a pair of very petite shoes: size four. He gazed above him at the huge sycamore tree that spanned the width of the road. Across one of its broad boughs, two thick ropes swayed in the night's light breeze. One noose would soon encircle the young man's neck. The other was for his partner, Curtis Hawley, who angrily scoffed when the Reverend D.W. Calfee offered to pray with the condemned men. "What the devil is the future to me," Hawley growled. "It's the present that's bothering me. I want to get away from this mob."

More than one hundred men watched as the diminutive Lafayette, barely out of his teens, unsteadily rose from the ground in his stocking feet. He had already fainted once and the crowd waited to see if he would die of fright before the noose did its work. When the order was given, dozens of hands willingly pulled the ropes that sent Lafayette V. Grime and Curtis B. Hawley to their deaths. Only four days prior, on August 20, 1882, they had enjoyed reputations as upstanding citizens in the town of Globe. Now they would forever be known as the most inept robbers and murderers in the young history of Arizona Territory.

Lafayette Grime, his older brother Cicero, and their friend Curtis Hawley were also three of the most unlikely road builders in Arizona. However, their attempt to construct a thoroughfare from the town of Pinal, just south of Globe, to the hamlet of Riverside, about 30 miles away, was the impetus that started them down the path to the ropes dangling from the sycamore tree.

Fair-haired Lafayette "Fate" Grime, a very slight man with unbelievably small feet, made his living tapping around Globe as a dance instructor. He supplemented his income by working in the mines and mills when money got tight on the dance floor. Cicero Grime, a photographer by trade, had recently established a construction company, Grime & Company, which was the operational base for their new venture. Curtis Hawley ran a wood and charcoal business providing materials to local mining companies.

The three men submitted a bid of $1,800 to build the wagon road, and their proposal was accepted on the condition they obtain a bond. Problem was, the road was going to cost about $4,000 to complete.

When they failed to secure a bond in the time allotted, the novice road builders requested and were given an extension until April 1, 1882. When that day came and went with no bond posted, the contract went to the next lowest bidder.

Undaunted, the men planned to build a bridge at the lower end of town. But as they talked through the logistics of such an undertaking, one of them suggested that robbing a stagecoach would be a lot easier and much more rewarding. From this casual remark, the three soon-to-be outlaws inaugurated plans to rob a Wells, Fargo shipment as the buckboard coach made its way through the Pinal Mountains from Casa Grande to Globe. These carriages often toted mail and payrolls of gold to local mines.

Not all stages were fully enclosed carriages. An open buckboard wagon was more adept at handling the rough road through the Pinals. Even then, trails to the mines deep within the mountains often required shipments be transferred to mule teams to maneuver the sometimes treacherous and often inaccessible pathways.

When the men heard a large shipment was coming through on Sunday, August 20, they headed about 4 miles into the mountains to Pioneer Pass where the road careened around a sharp bend. Lafayette and Curtis hunkered down behind a massive boulder and waited.

The bandits had no intention of shooting anyone, just slowing the mules and scaring the driver away. Along with Curtis's .44-caliber rifle and Lafayette's .50-caliber Springfield, they brought with them a miner's pickax and a hatchet, but no horses for the getaway.

Leaving his brother and Curtis behind the rock, Cicero, the spotter, steered his horse down the trail toward the expected payload. His job was to peacefully intercept the buckboard stage and determine if it carried a stash lucrative enough to warrant the holdup.

Muleskinner Frank Porter also waited for the Wells, Fargo wagon. As he steadied his six-mule team, he was glad to see Cicero Grime riding his way. Porter would transfer the heavy gold payroll to his mules for the ride up to the mining camp, and he was grateful to have Cicero's help to lighten the workload. As soon as the buckboard, driven by Wells, Fargo messenger Andy Hall, came to a halt, the men began hauling the gold off the wagon and onto the mules. Hall had already distinguished himself in Arizona history by serving with Major John Wesley Powell on the first successful trek through the Grand Canyon in 1869.

Curiosity got the better of Cicero as he tied the strongbox to Porter's lead mule. When Hall told him the box contained $5,000 in gold for the Mike Morris Mine, Cicero suppressed a satisfied sneer and quickly tightened the straps an extra notch. Picking up his horse's reins, he bade the two men so long and casually sauntered up the trail toward the hidden gunmen.

Reaching the boulder where Lafayette and Curtis lay in wait, Cicero alerted the men that the Wells, Fargo shipment contained a sizeable amount of gold and the heist was on. He warned that Hall, who was leading the pack train, had a gun, but that Porter, bringing up the rear, carried no weapon. Then Cicero headed back into Globe to give himself an alibi for the day's upcoming events.

Hall drove the mules cautiously. He knew one unsteady move would spook the creatures and he did not want any missteps until he delivered the hefty payload to the mine. As he approached the towering boulder, flanked by a steep incline on the other side of the trail, he slowed the mules to the pace of a well-fed snail.

Without warning Lafayette and Curtis opened fire, quickly killing the lead mule. Before Hall could react, another barrage of bullets sent him scurrying out of harm's way. He shouted to Porter, who had not yet reached the pass, to hightail it into Globe, and bring help—fast.

Hall hastily put greater distance between himself and the gunmen. Too far away to see them clearly, he assumed they were Indians since several Indian attacks had occurred recently in the vicinity. As he took aim, he saw two men slashing the ropes holding the strongbox to the now dead, treasure-laden mule. His shots missed but return fire found its mark and Hall hobbled away with a bullet through his thigh.

With his hatchet Lafayette hacked open the strongbox, swiftly transferred the money to his saddlebags, then swung the bags over his shoulder, ready to hightail it into the hills. Curtis wanted to sort through the registered mail for other lucrative loot, but Lafayette was already on the move, leaving the burly woodcutter to follow dutifully in the dancer's diminutive footsteps.

Before long, the two bandits came upon Dr. F.W. Vail who was leading a packhorse loaded with supplies to his mine. The well-respected Globe druggist had heard gunfire and asked the men if they knew what had happened. Lafayette and Curtis offered up that they suspected Indians were in the area and the three of them should press on together toward Globe. Vail unloaded his packhorse so the two horseless bandits could travel more expeditiously.

About a mile down the road, Lafayette and Curtis got jittery about Vail. They returned his horse and let the pharmacist get a few yards away before Curtis whipped out his gun and cowardly shot him in the back. Lafayette obligingly plugged a couple more bullets into the dying man.

Heading off on both of Vail's horses, the two men next ran into Hall who still believed Indians had attacked the mule team. Hall showed the bandits the bullet he had extracted from his thigh and urged them to join him in searching for the fugitives. Lafayette and Curtis agreed, but the novice desperadoes soon grew uneasy, particularly when Hall exhibited an increasing interest in Lafayette's overstuffed and very heavy saddlebags. Allowing Hall to get a few feet ahead, they opened fire. With his gun still in hand, Hall dropped dead to the ground; his trigger finger erratically sent a burst of gunfire into the air.

Not daring to take Dr. Vail's horses into Globe for fear the steeds would be recognized, the men headed out on foot, stopping only to divide the loot into three equal shares and bury it near Russell Gulch, each keeping a few of the $20 gold pieces for spending money. They then made their way, separately, back to town.

By now muleskinner Porter had arrived in Globe and sounded the alarm. Church bells rang out as a posse, headed by Gila County Sheriff William W. Lowther, took off into the mountains and the robbery site.

Around sundown, they came upon Dr. Vail, not far from death but able to identify his attackers as men he had seen around Globe: "one a big dark guy, the other a small fair-haired younger man."

Not much later the search party stumbled across Hall's body, sporting enough bullet holes to raise hairs on a rattlesnake's hide.

At the robbery site they quickly discovered the bandits' hiding spot and distinguished two sets of footprints behind the boulder, one so small they looked as if they belonged to a woman. From this shred of evidence, plus Dr. Vail's description of his assailants, the sheriff had a good idea who had committed the crimes. Only one man in town wore shoes that petite.

Within hours after the shooting, rewards totaling $6,000 were posted for the capture of the individual or persons responsible for the slayings of Dr. Vail and Andy Hall.

As the bodies of the two slain men were laid to rest on Monday, a mournful Cicero Grime volunteered to toll the bell for the funeral procession. Curtis decided the safest place for him was at home. Lafayette only stuck around long enough to return the rifle he had borrowed before heading for Wheatfields on the pretext of having work to do. Unfortunately, he forgot to clean the gun before returning it. The owner, somewhat suspicious of the condition of his rifle, took it to the gunsmith shop where the cartridges were compared with those found at the murder sites. The match was close enough to alert Sheriff Lowther.

On Tuesday, acting on Lowther's conviction that Lafayette was one of the men involved in the robbery and murders, Pete Gabriel, who served as both Pinal County Sheriff and U.S. Deputy Marshal, located the runaway suspect in Wheatfields. Wanting Lafayette to admit his part in the crime, the lawman did some fast talking to obtain the young man's confession.

Gabriel informed the inexperienced outlaw that he had witnessed the killing of Hall and saw Lafayette put three bullets in the poor man. Lafayette couldn't get the words out fast enough. "No, I didn't," he cried. "I only shot him twice." After that his confession was a mere formality, and he quickly implicated Curtis and Cicero. But he insisted his brother had nothing to do with the murders and only participated in the robbery.

By Wednesday all three men were under arrest. When Sheriff Lowther wired the Wells, Fargo agent in San Francisco that the culprits had been apprehended but the gold not yet recovered, the agent shot back, "Damn the money. Hang the murderers."

Marshal Gabriel wanted the suspects held in the Florence jail to be tried for tampering with the U.S. mail, but Sheriff Lowther argued the murders of Vail and Hall were more heinous crimes and insisted the men be locked up in Globe. Each of the lawmen may have had his eyes on the reward money, triggering a strong hankering to retain custody of the outlaws. At a deadlock, they finally agreed to let Judge J.D. McCabe determine which charge took precedence, and where the outlaws should be sequestered. The judge ordered the trio remanded into Sheriff Lowther's custody to stand trial for murder.

Tempers were running high in Globe by Wednesday evening. Retaliation for the two murdered men was the conversation running rampant through pristine parlors as well as in smoke-filled saloons. As hot blood permeated the town, Sheriff Lowther ordered all bars closed to allay any drunken violence, but it was too late.

Toward sundown, several hundred angry men assembled outside the jail, ready to break down the door if the sheriff did not turn over the three outlaws. They had already swung three ropes across the big sycamore tree in the middle of town.

Lowther insisted the outlaws be given a fair hearing. He sent for Justice of the Peace George Allen and moved his prisoners to Dr. Stallo's large dancehall to allow enough room for almost the entire town to witness the proceedings. Dr. Vail's widow, Irene, was there, along with Cicero's wife, Sylvia, and their four children.

Within minutes Judge Allen determined the prisoners be bound over to Superior Court for trial, but the crowd demanded instant retribution. They had already decided there would be a hanging that night.

Lafayette and Curtis agreed to show the mob where they had stashed the gold, hoping that might improve their dire situation. About thirty men marched the two desperadoes back to Russell Gulch to uncover the hidden treasure.

Meanwhile, Cicero was returned to his cell to await the outcome of the treasure hunt. His life would be spared thanks to the pleas of his wife and Mrs. Vail, both arguing he should be allowed to live since he took no part in the killings.

Returning to town with the loot and the condemned men, the assemblage refused to consider any more delays. As the church bells began to echo across the valley, Lafayette Grime and Curtis Hawley signed confessions and drew up their wills before the throng escorted them down the street to the sycamore tree.

It was now 2:00 A.M. Thursday. Two of the three ropes hanging from the tree were tightened and a dozen burly arms grabbed on to hoist the

Sycamore hanging tree in Globe used to hang Lafayette Grime and
Curtis Hawley.
Gila County Historical Society, Globe, Arizona, photo GM #36-2

men to their deaths. Only Lafayette's empty boots remained firmly on
the ground. The lifeless bodies remained on the sycamore tree until
almost noon before they were finally cut down. The four-day crime
spree resulted in four dead men, one dead mule, and Cicero Grime waiting in fearful expectation that another mob would determine he too
should hang.

On September 25, 1882, Cicero was tried and convicted of robbing
the U.S. mail and sentenced to serve twenty-one years in Yuma
Territorial Prison. He arrived in Yuma on October 11.

The following summer, Cicero started acting mighty strange and his
jailers became concerned he would harm himself or someone else with
his erratic behavior. Since Arizona would not build a facility for the
mentally ill until 1886, prison officials shipped him off to an asylum in
Stockton, California.

Two months after his arrival, Cicero walked out of the asylum and was never seen or heard from again. Speculation continues today as to whether he was really insane or faking his madness to get out of prison. In 1884 a man by the name of Robert Alexander was arrested in Oregon and accused of being the long-lost Cicero Grime, but no one could positively say he was the same man who had instigated the robbery in far-off Arizona, and he was released.

Peace returned to Globe until a devastating fire burned a large portion of the town in 1894, including the old sycamore hanging tree. Two years later, what remained of the tree was leveled to the ground. Whiskey-soaked old cowboys will tell you that when the wind whispers across the road where the majestic tree once stood, they can still hear the moans of condemned men who died under the massive sycamore branches. One has to listen hard, however, to hear the cries of Lafayette Grime and Curtis Hawley. They perpetrated their crimes so quickly and so futilely that they barely had time to confess before the tree enveloped them in the throes and satisfaction of vindication.

James Addison Reavis
The Noble Forger

Imagine walking into the state capital of Arizona and demanding ownership of more than twelve million acres of land spanning 235 miles west to east from Phoenix to the western boundaries of Silver City, New Mexico, and 75 miles north and south encompassing not only the Phoenix population but dozens of outlying agricultural and mining communities including Tempe, Mesa, Casa Grande, Florence, Safford, Globe, Miami, Superior, Clifton, Coolidge, and Morenci.

Five rivers run through this massive desert region and just as many Indian reservations occupy territory within its boundaries. The San Francisco and Mogollon Mountains jut out the eastern portion of the expanse with the Picacho, Galiuro, and Pinaleno Mountain ranges spanning the southern end.

Military enclaves fall within these boundaries and railroads run across the territory. Thousands of people occupy the land. Some claim less than an acre while others hold deeds to hundreds of acres that they farm, ranch, and mine. About 125 years ago, James Addison Reavis sought to claim all this land and everything that was on it as his own, and he almost got away with it.

Reavis was already in his thirties when he arrived in Arizona in 1880, but he had not been idle during his formative years. A Missourian by birth, he joined the Confederate Army at the age of eighteen but found military life dull and uninteresting. To keep himself occupied he practiced forging his commanding officer's signature and was soon handing out bogus leave papers and furloughs to his army buddies. When his ruse was discovered, he headed across the Mason-Dixon Line and enlisted in the Union Army. Boredom overtook him again. He asked for an official leave to marry and left the military, never to return. Neither did he marry.

Young Reavis spent a year in Brazil before settling in St. Louis around 1865 where he worked as a conductor on horse-drawn streetcars. He invested his meager earnings in land and property, never hesitating to produce a missing deed or document by falsifying the necessary papers. Soon his proclivity for fraud and forgery brought devious businessmen to his door. He gladly created counterfeit papers for those willing to pay for his talent.

In 1871 Doctor George M. Willing Jr. came looking for Reavis. Willing had abandoned his wife and children in St. Louis some years back to seek his fortune in the lucrative western goldfields. He claimed he had purchased a large tract of land in Arizona Territory from Miguel Peralta and his father, descendants of Spanish nobility who were now living in poverty. It was rich land, ripe for farming and ranching, and, according to his calculations, a wealth of gold and silver lay beneath the rocky soil. Would Reavis be interested in entering into a partnership to develop this valuable property?

Reavis listened intently as Dr. Willing described the bounty that awaited in Arizona. Whether he believed Willing or not, he saw opportunity far beyond what the good doctor envisioned and readily entered into the partnership. Willing headed west in late 1873. Reavis tarried long enough to marry Ada Pope on May 5, 1874, but left shortly thereafter and did not see Ada again for over six years. She divorced him in 1883, claiming desertion.

Reavis's route took him through the Isthmus of Panama into California. He arrived in San Francisco only to discover Willing had died in Prescott, Arizona, in March 1874. Willing's unclaimed gunnysack of belongings, including the deeds he said he had acquired from the Peralta heirs, was stowed in the coroner's attic in Prescott.

Reavis stayed in California for several years and taught school in Downey before hiring on as a subscription agent with the *San Francisco Daily Examiner.* During this time, he formulated a convoluted plan to make the best of his deal with the deceased Willing.

Reavis took the meager information Willing had related to him and set about creating a dynasty of enormous proportions. He knew that under the terms of the Treaty of Guadalupe Hidalgo (1848) and the Gadsden Purchase (1854), the United States was obligated to recognize valid Spanish and Mexican land grants. Most of the Arizona grants were considered worthless and had been abandoned by the original owners.

By now Reavis must have doubted that Miguel Peralta and his father even existed. Or if they did, they were far from the noble inheritors Willing had proclaimed them to be. He had seen enough forged documents in his day to figure out that the papers Willing had shown him were worthless. But those official-looking certificates, now reposing in the attic of the Prescott coroner's office, would become the impetus upon which he planned to defraud the people of Arizona out of millions of acres of land, and they must be dealt with. He had to obtain clear title to continue with his devious plot.

The Peralta Grant, as he decided to call it, would become property bequeathed to the family by proclamation of the King of Spain. Now all he had to do was create the Peralta clan, falsify existing records, and deposit these fraudulent documents where they could be "discovered" as evidence of the family's legal right to the land.

The family Reavis concocted began its reign in Spain in 1708 with the birth of Don Miguel Nemecio Silva de Peralta de la Córdoba. Don Miguel entered the service of the King of Spain and was sent to Guadalajara in New Spain (now Mexico) as a city inspector. Reavis gave him the title the Baron of Arizonaca and had the king bestow upon him a grant of land.

James Addison Reavis, "The Baron of Arizona."
Courtesy of Arizona Historical Society/Tucson, AHS #B112040

Don Miguel, according to Reavis, visited his northern tract of land only once, declaring the area around what is now Casa Grande the Barony of Arizona. Murderous Apaches purportedly drove him out of the region back to Mexico.

Don Miguel did not marry until he was sixty-two years old, Reavis claimed, but he soon had a son, Jesus Miguel Silva de Peralta de la Córdoba y Sanches de Bonilla, born in 1781. To eliminate the need for another generation, Reavis allowed Don Miguel to live to the age of 116. When he died, all his property went to Jesus Miguel. Under Reavis' penmanship, Jesus Miguel became the father of the miner who sold the Peralta lands to Dr. Willing. The Peraltas seemed to have long lifelines.

Reavis now had to get his hands on the deeds Willing had showed him in St. Louis.

When he stepped off the stagecoach in Phoenix in 1880, Reavis passed himself off as a reporter for the *Examiner*. Dressed in a long black coat and carrying a silver-knobbed cane, the tall, imposing man with sapphire blue eyes and a startling shock of red hair set out almost immediately for Prescott to locate the gunnysack Willing had left behind. He found the bag filled with Willing's clothing and odd items. At the very bottom lay the deeds signed by father and son, Jesus and Miguel Peralta. Reavis now had only one more person to eliminate in order to claim the Peralta property as his own.

Mary Ann Willing had known Reavis in St. Louis and trusted his friendship without reservation. So when Reavis promised her thousands of dollars if she would sign over to him her late husband's interest in the Peralta documents, she did not hesitate. Now with complete control of the false Peralta Grant, Reavis set about producing the documents he believed would convince the government of Arizona that the land grant actually existed.

With his penmanship expertise, he spent weeks perfecting forged documents. He re-created inks used in the 1700s and painstakingly practiced writing with the flourish of old Spanish monks and scribes. When he was satisfied with his masterpieces, he traveled to Spain and Mexico, surreptitiously inserting these well-crafted, ancient-looking papers into church records and official depositories verifying the existence of the Peralta family. At the same time, he furtively filched documents that disproved the existence of this noble clan.

All this planning and scheming took an enormous amount of time, effort, expertise, lying, cheating, and counterfeiting before Reavis felt he had established the Peralta lineage. By 1882 he was ready to lay claim to twelve million acres of prime Arizona land.

The man with the well-manicured mustache and sweeping side-burns who appeared in Tucson in March 1882 carried a suitcase brimming with "authentic" documents. He quickly hustled down the road to the Graham County courthouse in Safford to file papers asserting his legal ownership by purchase of the Peralta Grant. When the court refused to recognize his claim, Reavis returned to California to manufacture even more documents. In March 1883 he was back in Tucson filing a raft of deeds, documents, photographs, and conveyances with the U.S. surveyor general, claiming himself the rightful landowner to the twelve-million-acre Peralta Grant.

Reavis wasted no time collecting from those he insisted were usurping his land. He sold quitclaims to nervous farmers, ranchers, and settlers who were fearful of losing property they believed they already owned. They worried that if Reavis was the rightful owner, they would never obtain clear titles to their homes and properties unless they gave in to his demands. He requested little money from these landowners and often, for the price of a meal, he would give away a quitclaim or two. His purpose was to show that by signing the deeds, the good citizens of Arizona recognized his legal right to the land. Many were skeptical and refused to sign, but Reavis persevered in his quest for his "rightful" and "legal" property.

After it was reported the Southern Pacific Railroad had capitulated to his demands and agreed to pay $50,000 to continue building track across his property, Reavis felt he had the territory of Arizona up against a wall. But the papers he had filed with the surveyor general were under careful scrutiny.

In 1885 the court determined Reavis' claim was invalid. Tempers mounted against the stately gentleman. He fled to San Francisco with the *Weekly Phoenix Herald* proclaiming him the ". . . Earl of the Iron Jaw, Count of Confidence Land, Lord of the Limber Tongue and Great Mogul of the Territory. . . . Cheek thy name is Reavis!" He did not return for two years.

Reavis determined he needed a direct Peralta descendant to convince the courts the grant existed. He found his "angel" on the streets of California and transformed her into the Baroness of Arizona.

Sophia Treadway was born about 1864 to John and Kate Treadway, but they were long gone from her life when she ran into the devious Reavis. He sent her to a convent to become a lady and educate her in the refinements of royalty. In 1887 he introduced her to Tucson society as Doña Sophia Micaela Maso Reavis y Peralta de la Córdoba, his wife.

Reavis had to concoct the story of his wife's pedigree and place her within the Peralta dynasty. His fictional narrative proclaimed she was the great-granddaughter of the first Baron of Arizona. She had been born a twin but her brother died at birth and her mother shortly after. She was raised in Mendocino County, California, by her grandmother. Reavis said he first laid eyes on Doña Sophia while on a train and he immediately recognized her ancestral features as belonging to the Peralta clan.

When he was satisfied he had established Doña Sophia's royal birth, Reavis got out his ink pen to create the documents perfecting her lineage.

He set off once again on his well-traveled route to Spain and Mexico, leaving his newly crafted papers in the same depositories he had previously visited. When he returned to the states, he revealed documents "miraculously" found proving his wife's heritage, including the old will of Jesus Miguel bequeathing all his holdings, and particularly the Peralta land, to his granddaughter Doña Sophia.

In September 1887 Reavis, now calling himself James Addison Peraltareavis, filed the previously missing will with the Tucson office of the surveyor general. The *Arizona Daily Citizen* lamented, "It seems as if the woes of Arizona were never to end. First come the Apaches and then the blackmailers and land grabbers."

"Everything that I have done has been in the interest of my wife and not for any claim preferred by me," he told the *San Francisco Daily Examiner*. "I have nothing to do with it except in my character as her

[Doña Sophia's] husband. It is my duty to see that her rights are given her, and you can rest assured that I intend doing it."

While Reavis was busily counterfeiting, filching, and inserting the documents necessary to establish his argument that the Peralta Grant existed, Royal Johnson, the surveyor general, was working diligently to disprove the validity of the reams of papers filed by Reavis. In 1889 he reported his findings noting that many of Reavis' documents were written with a steel pen, an instrument not used until after 1800. He accurately pointed out the differences in penmanship between authenticated documents written in the 1700s and those filed by Reavis purportedly written at the same time. Paper watermarks appeared that were not available until the mid 1800s. There were misspellings of Spanish words in some of the fraudulent documents. Johnson ordered a search of Spanish archives for papers pertaining to the Peralta claim and found no evidence of the family. His report concluded with a recommendation that Reavis's claim be denied, "it being in my mind without the slightest foundation in fact and utterly void."

Reavis filed suit against the government, seeking damages in the amount of $10 million. He said the monies already paid to him proved the validity of his claim. Along with the Southern Pacific Railroad's $50,000, the Silver King Mining Company had handed over $25,000. In all, Reavis had already collected over $145,000 from landowners for the rights to use Peralta land, a sum equivalent to over $3 million today. Reavis brought his claim before the newly formed Court of Private Land Claims (established in 1891) in Santa Fe, New Mexico.

When court convened on June 3, 1895, Reavis was nowhere to be found, nor did he appear the next day, but the trial went forth without him. On June 5 the court received a telegram from Reavis asking the trial be continued until June 10.

Finally appearing and placed on the stand, Reavis proclaimed his sole desire in obtaining the Peralta Grant was "to develop Arizona. As a fact, I never cared that much for the grant, except the honor of having done something in it. I am not a lover of money, but I am a lover of development and building up a country. Therefore my whole life has been in the interest of building up Arizona . . ."

For two and a half days, he rambled on about the Peralta family. Then he wheeled a large truck into the courtroom that he claimed contained absolute proof of his wife's heritage. He began pulling copious amounts of documents out of the truck. Next came dozens of portraits, pictures of his wife's ancestors, he said. He argued this was all the proof the court should require to award his wife her rightful property. This is most likely the evidence he was creating when he was absent from court.

The court did not believe a word he said. His claim was deemed "wholly fictitious and fraudulent," and he was immediately arrested and charged with conspiracy to defraud the government.

Unable to provide bail, Reavis languished in jail for more than a year. His criminal trial commenced on June 27, 1896, and lasted just a few short days. Much of the same testimony presented at the first trial was again introduced. Witnesses who had initially backed Reavis's story now admitted they had lied. He was found "guilty as charged in the indictment to default the United States Government out of parts of its public lands in connection with the effort to establish the fictitious and fraudulent Peralta Grant."

Reavis's sentence was pretty mild considering he had hoped to acquire a good portion of Arizona Territory with his fraudulent scheme. He was sentenced to serve two years in the Santa Fe Penitentiary and pay a fine of $5,000. He promised he would appeal his conviction but never did. On April 18, 1898, he walked out of prison proclaiming he would once again "return to the world of business."

His wife, now using the name Sophia Treadway Reavis, and no longer asserting her noble status, settled in Denver with the couple's twin boys, Miguel and Carlos, born in 1893, and their adopted son, Fenton. In 1902 she filed for divorce, citing desertion and nonsupport. Reavis languished in California, never again experiencing the opulent

James Addison Reavis in prison.
Courtesy of Arizona State Library, Archives and Public Records, Archive Division, #97-7968

lifestyle he enjoyed as an Arizona aristocrat. Penniless, he took up residency in the Los Angeles County Poor Farm but moved to Denver in 1914. He died on November 20, 1914.

No other criminal came close to robbing Arizona of the vast sums of money and millions of acres of land that James Addison Reavis tried to swindle. He was a brilliant and talented man who lived a life of fraud and fantasy. His scheme to be acknowledged as a nobleman earned him only one thing, the dubious title of the Baron of Arizona.

Charles P. Stanton
The Puppetmaster

The eight desperadoes rose from the desert floor like a deadly mirage in the torrid July heat, descending on the lone wagon as it made its way along the sun-baked road. With little fanfare they grabbed the driver and stabbed him to death as his family watched in horror. As the mother and her two young sons frantically pleaded for their lives, a bald-headed man with no eyebrows or eyelashes grabbed the woman by the hair and held her head back while another quickly slit her throat. Within seconds the boys met the same fate. Wasting no time, the men methodically scalped their victims, tossed the bodies into the wagon, confiscated a strongbox, and set fire to the carriage, obliterating all traces of the Barney Martin family.

From a nearby hilltop a man watched as the massacre went down, the smell of burning flesh not at all unpleasant to him. An evil smirk played across his smarmy face as the eight men rode up the hill and dropped the strongbox at his feet. Taking his share of the loot, Charles P. Stanton headed back to Antelope Station, a small mining community near Wickenburg, Arizona. He stashed his plunder in a secluded spot, poured himself a glass of the finest Irish whiskey, and toasted his success. He had just masterminded a reprehensible crime without getting any blood on his lily-white hands.

When the remains of the Martin family were found on August 8, 1886, almost three weeks after they had disappeared, only a few bone fragments were left to bury.

Charles P. Stanton, the man who had instigated this atrocious crime, preferred the title Lord Stanton, claiming he was the son of an Irish

Charles Stanton standing outside his store.
Sharlot Hall Museum Photo, Prescott, Arizona

aristocrat. Of course there is no proof of his lineage, just as there would be no proof he perpetrated some of the vilest offenses in Arizona history.

As a young man, Stanton attended Dublin's Trinity College and entered Monmouth Monastery in England to study for the priesthood. However, he was expelled from Monmouth, either for stealing from the coffers or for immoral acts. Whatever the reason, he departed England for America with a bounty of £1,000 on his head.

Few records exist of Stanton's first few years in the United States, but he was probably in his mid-thirties when he filed for U.S. citizenship in New York City in 1864. By the time his petition was granted on August 26, 1872, he was already creating a westward path of destruction.

He may have been involved in the John Slack and Philip Arnold Diamond Hoax that erupted across the country in 1872. Two prospectors had liberally salted the Wyoming hills with inferior diamonds and rubies and passed them off as valuable precious stones just waiting to be plucked from the ground. Wealthy, intelligent people spent millions of dollars investing in this fraudulent scheme, never believing a couple of destitute miners could outsmart them. Some believe Stanton may have gotten his hands on a sizeable amount of the profits from this venture. No proof exists of his involvement, but chances are, he was running from the law when he arrived in Arizona Territory in the early 1870s.

He went to work as an assayer and gemologist for Sexton White, owner of the Vulture Mine near Wickenburg. After the mine closed down, he continued to analyze prospectors' ore findings, usually with some of the gold dust ending up in his pocket, the miner no wiser than a blind owl.

Stanton settled in Antelope Station at the base of Rich Hill, where one of the richest deposits of placer gold was discovered in 1863. Prospectors dug out more than 10,000 gold nuggets in just a few months and the mountain continued to yield its wealth over the next few years. By the time Stanton showed up, however, the mountaintop had little left to offer. Miners still clung to the hope of finding another big lode, but most turned to farming and ranching for their livelihoods. Antelope Creek and the nearby Hassayampa River provided ample nourishment for crops and cattle.

Pioneer ranchers Charles and Ida Genung, well respected in the Wickenburg area, were impressed with the sophisticated and knowledgeable assayer and welcomed Stanton into their home to educate their three daughters. It wasn't long, however, before the girls complained their new tutor touched them inappropriately. Never one to waste words or actions, Ida grabbed her pistol and ordered the Irishman out of her house never to return. From then on, Charles Genung kept a close watch over Stanton's dealings.

By 1875 Antelope Station contained a five-stamp mill, a boardinghouse, and about a dozen houses. A post office was established and Stanton was elected postmaster, although many of the names that showed up on the election ballots were also found on nearby grave-stones, leading many to suspect the new postmaster had rigged the election. Before long he had also accepted the duties of deputy sheriff and justice of the peace, then proceeded to rename the town. Antelope Station became known as Stanton, Arizona Territory. The new name lasted about six months before voters were able to reestablish the community as Antelope Station.

Two men ran rival stage stops and stores in the bustling township, competing for business from stagecoaches making their way to and from Phoenix, Prescott, and the Colorado River towns. Storeowner Yaqui Wilson endeared himself to hungry passengers by raising his own beef and hogs and preparing hearty meals greedily devoured after a tedious journey. Plus, his home-brewed whiskey, well known and desired throughout the territory, was always a thirst-quencher after a dusty ride. But when the stage company added a barn to house and feed its horses near Englishman William Partridge's place, coaches no longer stopped at Wilson's establishment. The passengers, however, preferring Wilson's food to Partridge's less-than-edible vittles, often got off at Partridge's and walked the half-mile to Wilson's to eat. There was no love lost between the two men.

Stanton also set up a general store, but most people preferred to avoid the often rude and offensive shopkeeper. What Stanton really wanted was the lucrative stagecoach business benefiting the other two establishments. Befriending both men, he devised a malevolent scheme to eliminate his competition.

Whoever let Wilson's hogs loose knew exactly where they would head. The porkers loved the bucknut shrubbery and prickly pear fruit that covered Partridge's property. However, the swine did not know the outside from the inside and invaded Partridge's house, creating a considerable mess. Aware of the escalating feud between the two men, Stanton judiciously advised Wilson to apologize to Partridge for his swines' behavior and to pay for what had been ruined. Out of the other side of his mouth, he informed Partridge that Wilson was out to kill him.

Rifle in hand, Partridge met up with the apologetic Wilson and shot him before the poor man could utter a word. When Partridge realized Wilson had come to him unarmed, he fled into the desert. Following the fugitive, Stanton persuaded Partridge to turn himself in. At the trial Stanton testified against the woeful Englishman, solidifying the poor man's conviction for second-degree murder. On November 2, 1877, Partridge was sentenced to life in the Yuma Territorial Prison.

With his two rivals now out of the way, Stanton became the most powerful man in Antelope Station. He was ready to step in and take over the two businesses abandoned by the death of Wilson and incarceration of Partridge. However, Wilson had a partner, John Timmerman, who decided to run the dead man's store. Partridge's creditors hired Barney Martin to run the other station. Stanton was furious he had lost out on these two lucrative holdings and decided he needed more muscle.

Francisco Vega (or Valenzuela), a big, ugly man with little hair anywhere on his head, led a band of desperadoes who enjoyed a reign of terror over central Arizona, looting and killing at will. They made their headquarters in Weaver, a nearby ramshackle mining settlement that catered to renegades and criminals. Travelers, fearing for their lives, often avoided this part of the country. Stanton hired the malevolent outlaws whenever he needed a particularly cruel or vindictive deed accomplished. He was about to use their expertise against his competitors.

The inexperienced Timmerman had gratefully accepted Stanton's offer to assist him with the store's books, so when Timmerman set out for Wickenburg one day, he told Stanton he had $700 in gold dust with him to pay off a San Francisco merchant. As Timmerman sauntered down the dusty road to Wickenburg, Juan Reval, one of Vega's men, suddenly appeared beside him. With little conversation between the two men, Reval shot Timmerman through the heart, relieved him of the gold he carried, doused the body in oil, and set it on fire. Stanton watched the slaying from a safe distance. He and Reval split the proceeds of the heist, adding to Stanton's blood-money stash. At the time no evidence linked Stanton to the crime.

Appointing himself appraiser of Timmerman's estate, Stanton also named himself the storeowner's sole beneficiary. He had accomplished half of what he set out to do. Now only the Martin family stood in his way.

When Barney Martin started receiving death threats, he initially dismissed them as pranks. But then his barn burned down, and soon after his house lay in a heap of smoldering cinders. He rebuilt the house, but as he again watched it go up in flames, he saw Stanton running from the fire. Grabbing his rifle, Barney took aim but his gun had been tampered with and did not go off. Disgusted and distraught, he knew he had to get his family out of harm's way. Martin sold his property for $5,000 and set out that hot July day in 1886 for a new beginning in Phoenix.

The two-day trip was eased by an overnight visit with friends, and Barney expected Charles Genung to accompany him on the road into Phoenix. But Genung had been delayed on business and never met up with the Martins. As Barney steered his horses along the well-rutted road, Mrs. Martin kept her eye on their two boys, ages nine and eleven, bouncing about in the rear of the wagon, their clothes covered in layers of road dust. She despaired of ever getting them clean again.

Stanton knew Martin carried the money from the sale of his property. As one of Vega's men later confessed, Stanton hired the outlaws to eliminate all traces of the Martin family, insisting they make the massacre look like the work of raiding Indians. Elano Hernandez, one of the vilest men to walk the earth, ordered Barney out of the wagon and slit his throat before Martin could grab his gun.

Genung knew Stanton was behind the killings and would not let the investigation rest in the hands of lawmen who were under the Irishman's control. As his grandson, Dan B. Genung, would later write, his grandfather went to see Mrs. McGinnis, who often cooked for the Vega gang.

She claimed the killers got drunk one night and bragged about the murders. They laughed, she said, when they described how Mrs. Martin, who had often cared for Vega's wife and four children, pleaded with the outlaws to spare her and the children. As she clung to his knees begging for their lives, Vega thanked the distraught woman for her kindness to his family, then grabbed her hair so Hernandez could slit her throat. The boys shortly lay beside their mother. The outlaws' only disappointment, said Mrs. McGinnis, was that Genung was not with the Martin family as expected. Stanton wanted Genung out of the way; the rancher had become too suspicious of the Irishman's covert activities.

Stanton reveled in the authority and power he now held over the town. Even the *Tombstone Epitaph* described the little burg as "bloody Stanton." Disasters haunted the district but no one could touch Lord Stanton.

After a rancher refused to buy supplies from Stanton's store because his prices were too high, the cattleman found himself watching helplessly as his property went up in flames. A safe distance away, Stanton warmed himself from the heat of the fire.

Two cattlemen caught Francisco Vega trying to set fire to their ranch house. They lectured the outlaw, told him never to come near their property again, and let him go. Shortly a large grass fire forced the ranchers to relocate more than 1,400 head of cattle hundreds of miles away to Tombstone. Vega and Stanton enjoyed a good laugh and a stiff drink as the cowboys herded their cattle out of town.

Back in 1870 Dennis May had discovered the profitable Leviathon gold mine. Stanton told May not to worry about filing the proper yearly paperwork to keep the mine in May's name. As justice of the peace, he would handle it. But Stanton never filed the annual assessments and eventually threatened to report May if the prospector didn't give up half interest in one of the most lucrative gold mines in the district. An irate May was so disgusted over his forced partnership with Stanton that he sold his remaining interest in the mine for a mere $10,000.

About the same time the Martin family disappeared, E.O. Grant's store in Wickenburg almost went up in flames when someone threw a ball of oil-saturated cotton through the shed window where several barrels of oil and liquor were stored. Tracks led to the Vulture Mill and then toward Stanton's place.

Charles Genung experienced Stanton's vindictiveness when one of his houses burned down.

But the worst devastation occurred when young girls crossed Stanton's path. More than one bore the marks of his brutality; some disappeared after run-ins with the debaucher. Fourteen-year-old Froilano Lucero survived a vile attack perpetrated by Stanton but her brothers demanded satisfaction for their sister's honor.

Pedro Lucero and his brother watched one day as the burly Stanton headed down the road. Pedro took aim and fired but his bullet only nicked the Irishman's ear. His brother missed altogether. Irate over the attack, Stanton offered a $5,000 reward for Pedro, dead or alive. He also issued warrants for the entire town of Weaver, certain he would catch some of the Lucero family in his net. But when he could not locate his ear-piercing enemy, he swore out a warrant for Pedro's father. Under Stanton's orders, deputies arrested the frail sixty-year-old and beat him senseless as they escorted him into Prescott and locked him up. He was eventually released when Genung paid his bail.

In September 1886 Juan Reval, serving time on an unrelated charge, confessed he had murdered Timmerman on Stanton's orders. He also admitted his part in a stage robbery that netted three gold bars, one of which ended up in Stanton's hands. Already the prime suspect behind the Martin murders after another of Vega's men, an Indian, confessed to following Stanton's orders in the brutal attack, Lord Stanton was arrested and taken to Phoenix. But the testimony of a convicted felon and an Indian outlaw were not enough to keep him behind bars. No concrete evidence materialized linking Stanton with any of the crimes of which he was accused and he was released. He boldly rode out of town on one of Barney Martin's horses.

On the evening of November 13, 1886, as he often did on a Saturday night, Stanton closed the door of his store and offered a drink to one of his cronies named Kelly (or Kelley). As they nipped at their whiskey, they heard horses ride up. Three men stood politely in the doorframe requesting directions to Walnut Grove and asking if they could camp nearby for the night. They also wanted to buy some tobacco. Stanton invited the men inside and went behind the counter to retrieve the smokes. As he turned toward the men, one of them aimed straight at Stanton's heart and did not miss.

The three Lucero brothers fled as Kelly opened fire; one never made it out of the yard. Some say Kelly killed the man while others believe he was hit with a bullet from one of his own brothers' guns.

No one bothered to investigate, much less arrest, the individuals who had ended the life of Charles P. Stanton. Everyone sighed in relief and gave thanks Lord Stanton was no longer the aristocratic puppetmaster who controlled the strings of power in the tiny hamlet of Antelope Station.

News also spread that Francisco Vega, the bald-headed man with no soul, had escaped into Mexico, although Charles Genung later heard the outlaw had been gunned down near Wickenburg running from a stage-coach robbery.

In 1895 mining engineer George Upton bought the town of Antelope Station, but its population was rapidly declining. For unknown reasons in 1896, the community voted to return the town's name to Stanton. As the Great Depression raged across the country in the late 1920s, the mining community experienced a small revival when dozens of out-of-work, hungry men set up lean-to shacks and tents and tried to eke out a living working old placers.

Over the years the old post office opened and closed as often as a saloon door. Shut down in 1890 it reopened in 1894. By 1905 the town fell into a permanent downhill demise and the post office was officially discontinued. The town never again experienced the days when gold and Charles P. Stanton were its masters.

In 1959 Upton's niece, who had acquired the town after her uncle's death, sold part of Stanton to the *Saturday Evening Post* magazine. It would be the grand prize in a jingle contest. The rest of the town was eventually sold to the Lost Dutchman Mining Association.

Today Charles Stanton's legacy can be found scattered among a few old adobe buildings, an infinite assortment of prickly pear cactus, overgrown weeds, languishing desert blooms, and a scattering of tombstones. Stanton's grave, however, lies about a mile outside of town in a desolate canyon circled by watchful vultures. He is not wanted in the town that bears his name.

The Apache Kid
Army Scout, Apache Rebel

O n May 3, 1887, the earth trembled across southwestern United States territory and northern Mexico. The earthquake, estimated at about 7.2 magnitude, lasted a full minute with massive rocks careening down mountains and huge fissures dashing jaggedly across the desert terrain, sending adobe homes crashing to the ground. Newspapers reported "deep rumblings" in the desert near the town of Superior, Arizona, where ". . . large pieces of rock were detached on all sides of Picket Post Mountain . . . raising a cloud of dust, and for several minutes it ascended about the mountain giving it the appearance of a live volcano."

About 20 miles east of Superior, Apache Indians, forced to live on the San Carlos Indian Reservation, believed that earthquakes foretold the onset of doom and disaster. To alleviate their fears, they gathered to brew *tizwin*, a potent, fermented mixture combining the heart of the maguey or mescal plant with fruits and vegetables. The ensuing *tizwin* party altered the lives of many Apaches that day, but the life of Has-kay-bay-nay-ntayl, known to the whites as the Apache Kid, or Kid for short, was changed beyond redemption.

A trusted Indian scout with the white man's army on the San Carlos Indian Reservation, the Apache Kid knew his people were forbidden to brew the intoxicating *tizwin*, but as he was mourning the slaying of his father, Toga-de-Chuz, he joined the illegal gathering. Toga-de-Chuz's murderer, Gon-zizzie, had been killed by Toga-de-Chuz's friends, but as the eldest son, Kid was expected to avenge his father's death in his own way.

Prison photo of Apache Kid taken in 1888 at Globe, Arizona.
Courtesy of the Arizona Historical Society/Tuscon, AHS #15755

Kid drank his share of the liquor and was soon plotting to kill Rip, the brother of Gon-zizzie. He enlisted his half brother, As-ki-say-la-ha, who was also an Indian scout, and the two rode off to roust three more scouts before setting out to find Rip.

Rip stood no chance against Kid's precise aim—he was dead before he hit the ground. Their mission a success, Kid and the four scouts returned to the reservation. They had been gone without permission for five days. Al Sieber, chief of the Indian scouts, had been looking for his wayward men.

For the most part, Sieber managed his troop of Indian scouts with an iron hand and a compassionate heart, but trouble spewed across his face when the scraggly group appeared before him. Sieber demanded their weapons and Kid was the first to obey. A crowd gathered as Sieber ordered the men arrested and locked in the guardhouse—a smelly, bug-infested hole furnished with only a handful of straw and a bucket.

Suddenly shots rang out from the crowd, and Sieber, unarmed, fell to the ground with a bullet embedded in his ankle. Seizing the opportunity, Kid grabbed a horse and fled the ensuing melee. He did not intend to lose his freedom for avenging his father's death, something he was compelled to do according to Apache law. As he turned his back on the white man's rules and laws, his days as a trusted Indian scout were over.

Has-kay-bay-nay-ntayl was born around 1860 near the Aravaipa Canyon in eastern Arizona. A loose translation of his name, "brave and tall and will come to a mysterious end," seemed to predict his calamitous future.

Has-kay-bay-nay-ntayl was forced onto the San Carlos Indian Reservation, as were many Indians, through the actions of President Ulysses S. Grant, who established San Carlos in 1872. The government determined that the only way to control warring Apaches was to confine them to reservations where they were expected to raise crops instead of raiding nearby ranches. Has-kay-bay-nay-ntayl's father was a member of Capitán Chiquito's band of White Mountain Apaches, who in 1875 were herded onto the dry, desolate reservation aptly called "Hell's Forty Acres."

As a teenager, Has-kay-bay-nay-ntayl seemed to adapt to reservation living. He learned to speak English and shunned the traditional dress of his father, opting to wear suit jackets, felt hats, and leather boots—white man's clothing. On the reservation he was in charge of shooting cattle as they came into the pens for slaughter and he became an expert marksman by running along fence lines surrounding the cattle pens while taking dead aim on the doomed creatures. He also herded cattle for ranchers in the nearby town of Globe. When white men found his name too hard to pronounce, they dubbed him Kid.

Around 1879 Al Sieber made this cocky nineteen-year-old his orderly and cook. With Sieber's encouragement Kid enlisted as an Indian scout in 1881 and reenlisted seven times until 1887. He often took time off between reenlistments, and during one of these respites, he married and had a child.

The military quickly promoted Kid to first sergeant, a rank he held during most of his enlistment, when they discovered how accurately he could spot distant riders and decipher whether they were whites or Indians. He was considered better than any military posse at tracking down runaway Indians, and Sieber often relied on him to help train new Indian scouts. In 1882 he fought in the Battle of Big Dry Wash on the Tonto Rim near the town of Payson, and he accompanied Sieber into Mexico during the 1885 Geronimo campaign.

He did not always toe the military line, however. In Mexico in late 1885, he almost got himself killed when he and two other scouts were accused of molesting a Mexican woman. As the scouts fled, shots rang out—one dead, one wounded, and Kid arrested. Mexican authorities feared an international incident if they tried the scout, so they released him back to the States after charging him a $25 fine.

When Sieber departed San Carlos for Fort Apache on an inspection trip just before that fateful day in May 1887, he left Kid in charge of the

Indian scouts. *Tizwin* and trouble soon merged into the incident that found the Apache Kid a renegade outlaw hunted by the very scouts he had trained.

About a dozen rebels fled the reservation along with Kid, and his band increased in numbers as days turned into weeks. When two ranchers were found dead near Benson, their cattle butchered and horses long gone, word spread that the runaway Indians were the culprits.

As the posse closed in, the Indians surrendered. On June 25, 1887, Kid and the four Indian scouts who had ridden with him to avenge his father's death were tried for mutiny and desertion in a general court-martial. Kid wasted no time admitting his guilt:

> I am 1st Sergeant Kid, San Carlos, Arizona Territory. God sent bad spirit in my heart, I think. You all know all the people can't get along very well in the world. There are some good people and some bad people amongst them all. I am not afraid to tell all these things because I have not done very much harm. I killed one man whose name is Rip because he killed my father. I am not educated like you and therefore can't say very much. If I had made any arrangement before I came in, I would not have given up my arms at Mr. Sieber's tent. That is all I have to say.

At the end of the day, all five scouts were found guilty and sentenced to death by shooting. When military commander General Nelson A. Miles reviewed the case, he requested leniency for the men, arguing they were "ignorant, unlettered Indians . . .," and while their deeds were certainly serious, they were "not of that extreme gravity which would justify the death sentence." The same court that had condemned them to death reduced their sentences to life in prison at Fort Leavenworth, Kansas.

For six months the Indians languished in the fetid San Carlos jail. On January 23, 1888, orders arrived transferring them not to Leavenworth Military Prison but to Alcatraz Island, California.

Completed shortly before Kid's arrival, Alcatraz boasted 185 wooden cells with 2-inch plank flooring covered in sheet iron. The only ventilation in each cell came from a 4-inch gap above the door and a meager 2-inch space below. Fire was always a concern and in March 1888, while Kid was at Alcatraz, a blaze destroyed several buildings.

The five ex-scouts were freed from Alcatraz in October 1888 when Judge Advocate General G. Norman Lieber successfully argued that the white jury that had convicted them was prejudiced against the Apaches and the sentences handed down were too harsh for the crimes committed.

Al Sieber was so angry when the Apache Kid reappeared at San Carlos that he immediately ordered him rearrested. He charged Kid with attempted murder, claiming his once-trusted scout had fired the bullet that shattered his ankle. Sieber conveniently ignored the fact that Kid had handed over his gun before the shooting started. He also disregarded the time Kid had already served for the San Carlos incident and ordered Gila County Sheriff Glenn Reynolds to lock the former scout in the Globe jail. "That evening," according to Apache Kid biographer Phyllis de la Garza, "bells clanged in the wooden tower of the Methodist church, Globe's customary practice signifying bad Indians were in town."

Sieber swore under oath that Kid had fired the shot that left him crippled for life. On October 30, 1889, the Apache Kid was sentenced to seven years in the Yuma Territorial Prison for the attempted murder of his mentor. Two days later he was on his way to Yuma.

Threatening rain clouds hovered overhead that All Saints Day as eight handcuffed Apache convicts shuffled out of the Globe jail and boarded the stagecoach for Yuma Prison. Stagecoach driver Eugene Middleton rubbed the dust off his brand new, heavy-duty, bright green Concord stagecoach with sunny yellow wheels as he watched the men board. Sheriff Reynolds and his deputy, William "Hunkydory" Holmes, would escort the prisoners. Kid climbed into the coach and Reynolds secured leg irons on the man considered the most dangerous of his charges.

The stage would carry the prisoners to Casa Grande, a two-day trip from Globe. From there, they would board a train for the final trek into Yuma.

Rain started falling before the stage skidded into the Riverside station for the night. After supper the prisoners lined up on benches, their leg irons and handcuffs securely tightened. In this upright position, they tried to sleep.

The next morning the stage had to maneuver the wet and slippery Kelvin Grade, and Middleton feared the coach, laden with passengers, would not make it up the muddy incline. Reynolds ordered the prisoners out of the coach—all except the Apache Kid and another convict shackled to him. Reynolds did not want Kid footloose.

Middleton maneuvered the stage as Reynolds and Holmes escorted the prisoners on foot up Kelvin Grade. The Apaches talked among themselves but since neither Reynolds nor Holmes spoke their language, their conversations were nothing more than gibberish to the two lawmen. Too bad for them.

As the stagecoach disappeared around a bend, two prisoners attacked Reynolds while two more grabbed Holmes. Both men died instantly with bullet wounds from their own rifles.

One of the prisoners ran toward the stage and fired at Middleton, sending him tumbling from the coach with a bullet through his mouth and neck. As the prisoners freed Kid and his companion, one angry Indian stood over the paralyzed Middleton ready to smash his head with a rock. For some reason, Kid stopped the man and spared Middleton's life. The Indians disappeared on foot across the desert plain and into the hills they knew so well.

News of the murders spread rapidly. The *Silver Belt* reported bloody clothing was found a few miles from the murder scene. "A carcass of a steer was also discovered, a part of which had been taken and some of the hide stripped off and used for foot-covering, as evidenced by the peculiar tracks made by one of the fugitives after leaving the spot."

Al Sieber assumed Kid had orchestrated the deadly escape and requested military posses to capture his nemesis. Five Arizona forts responded with troops tracking the fugitives' trail of destruction.

Although the prisoners were on foot and most were unarmed, the posses were no match for the elusive Apaches. Once, Kid was spotted near the San Carlos River, but he quickly vanished into the hills. Another time, a posse found a cave where the Indians camped, but they magically disappeared as the law closed in. The fugitives raided ranches and stole horses, then headed farther into the mountains.

Territorial Governor Lewis Wolfley offered a $500 reward for the conviction of any of the outlaw Apaches. Still, no one could catch the swift-footed renegades, who were obviously making their way toward Mexico.

The Apache Kid and the men who followed him became the most feared Indians in Arizona history. Ranchers were gunned down, their cattle butchered, and horses stolen. Cowboys were found with their heads split open. In March 1890 a freight hauler was murdered near Fort Thomas. That August, three men were killed at Hachita, about 50 miles southwest of Lordsberg, New Mexico. Even western artist Frederick Remington feared crossing Kid's path. While looking for a lost mine in Sonora, Mexico, Remington noted, "The vaqueros I am riding with are not only looking for the lost mine of Tiopa, but are also primed for a fight with the Kid if we cut his trail. And if he cuts ours, we may not live long enough to regret it."

Eventually five of the original eight Apache prisoners were captured; two others, killed. By October 1890 only Kid remained free. The *Silver Belt* considered him "a legal target for those who can cock a gun and draw a bead through the sights of a Winchester."

That December, three ranch hands killed an Indian they found butchering one of their steers. From the nearby brush Kid and his men came out shooting. The cowboys took shelter behind a large boulder, and gunfire resounded across the hillside for hours until one of the ranch hands barely dodged a bullet that shattered his corncob pipe. His two buddies, amused at his startled expression, carelessly leaned out from behind their boulder refuge. One was stopped in mid-laugh by a bullet in the head, and it wasn't long before the second cowboy lay dead. The pipe-smoking gunman headed for the nearest ranch, successfully eluding Kid and his men, but chances are he never lit up a pipe again.

In 1891 an ex-army scout said he chanced upon the Apache Kid in the Santa Catalina Mountains about 20 miles north of Tucson. Neither man backed off and all day the two sat facing each other, their eyes never leaving the gaze of their adversary, knowing either could kill with one shot. Along about sundown, Kid rose from his rock and announced he was leaving. "As Kid disappeared down the trail, I lit a shuck for home!" the old scout recalled years later.

Occasionally Kid returned to the San Carlos Indian Reservation to retrieve bundles of food, clothing, and ammunition secreted in caves by his family and sympathetic friends. He often took a woman with him when he departed once again for the hills. Some of these women went willingly, while others had no choice.

By November 1892 Territorial Governor Nathan Oakes Murphy upped the reward to $6,000 for the capture or death of the Apache Kid. Several Arizona counties offered their own rewards; and since he was blamed for murders in New Mexico Territory as well as south of the border, additional reward money resulted in an accumulated total of $15,000 on his head. Still, no one came near arresting the elusive Indian.

In 1894 Al Sieber, maybe having a change of heart after falsely accusing his trusted scout of attempted murder, tried to get word to Kid that if he would turn himself in, Sieber would help clear his name with the reward money. Sieber waited at several designated spots for Kid to appear, but he never did.

The December 1895 day was bone-chillingly cold as Horatio Merrill and his daughter Eliza steered their wagon from Pima toward the town of Clifton. About six miles from Ash Springs, they were attacked and slain. Lawmen believed at least thirty Indians, led by the Apache Kid, had set upon the pair. When they found the Indians' campsite, they discovered Eliza Merrill's purse; nestled inside, her newly acquired engagement ring lay undisturbed.

As years passed, tales of the Apache Kid's death began to sprout as often as the offenses laid at his feet. From about 1895 until the mid 1930s, just about everyone had a story to tell. He was found dead in a cave, killed in a cornfield, ambushed at a waterhole, shot off his horse, and slain by Mexican *rurales*.

Arizona pioneer Charles Genung said Kid appeared at his Wickenburg campsite in 1895 obviously dying from consumption. That same year, rancher John Slaughter supposedly followed Kid into Mexico and killed him.

In 1899 the chief of the Mexican *rurales* claimed Kid was living peacefully in the Sierra Madre Mountains.

In 1915 Kid supposedly rode with Pancho Villa, rebel general of the Mexican Revolution.

A nephew of Kid, Joe Adley, said his uncle was still alive in Mexico in 1924. And as late as about 1935, an old cattleman swore he had recently talked with Kid, who claimed he and his family were living in Mexico. After that, the stories stopped.

"Torn between bewildering laws in a white man's world and old Apache tribal traditions, [the Apache Kid] tried adapting to both, and lost," wrote de la Garza. Freedom to live his life according to Apache custom was all Has-kay-bay-nay-ntayl wanted. The price of that freedom cost him dearly.

Wham Paymaster
——Robbery——
The Cattlemen's Caper

In the dim light of dawn, thirteen-year-old Andy Carlson watched wide-eyed as the men tied rags over their horses' mouths to muffle the snorts and whinnies that would surely give them away. For several days the gang had been living in a stifling hot cave surviving on sardines and deviled ham as they erected buttresses above the road that led from Fort Grant to Fort Thomas in southeastern Arizona. This afternoon, the army paymaster would come down this road carrying a payroll close to $30,000. The men had no intention of letting him get to Fort Thomas with his bounty. Young Andy, who would stay behind and hold the horses during the upcoming battle, remembered the events of May 11, 1889, the rest of his life, and he often bragged of his involvement in the greatest military robbery in Arizona history.

Some of the manmade barricades along the ridge were so large that five or six men could hide behind them. Towering sporadic boulders added additional protection. To give the illusion of even more gun power on the hilltop, the men carved yucca stalks to look like rifles, then positioned them along the breastworks aimed at the road below. Their final task was to push a huge boulder across the road to block the soldiers' march to Fort Thomas.

At least a dozen men may have been on the hilltop that warm May day, but only seven local cattlemen would be tried for the crime.

Chauncey Gilbert Webb Jr., known as Gilbert, was the likely ringleader of the holdup gang. At age fifty-three he was certainly the oldest participant. He and his sons ran the Webb Cattle Company along with several other businesses near the Mormon community of Pima. Gilbert was a leader in the Church of Jesus Christ of Latter-day Saints, even though an affair with a local widow caused his name to be stricken from church rolls. Gilbert fell on hard times during the late 1800s and was forced to sell many of his holdings. At the time of the payroll robbery, he was suspected of illegal cattle branding. At least one of his sons, Wilfred, accompanied his father into the encampment above the road to Fort Thomas.

Mark E. Cunningham also owned a ranch and was eagerly wooing a local gal. He had served as a Graham County deputy sheriff, but lost his bid for sheriff in 1888. His proclivity for gambling may have led to his desire to acquire the army payroll.

Brothers Lyman and Warren Follett, who had a spread nearby, were fingered as part of the robbery gang, along with David Rogers and Thomas Norman Lamb, cowhands on the Webb ranch. All of these men had ties to the Mormon Church except for the gambler, Mark Cunningham.

Mormons had settled the thriving community of Pima along the Gila River in 1879. By the late 1800s, however, ranchers saw their livelihoods shriveling under the desert sun and government taxes. Eastern factions controlled Arizona's purse strings, and the glut of military posts in the territory meant thousands of dollars that could have helped desperate ranchers went into military coffers instead. Discontent was also brewing in religious sectors. Non-Mormons resented the power of the Mormon Church, particularly its influence in local elections. On the other hand Mormons bristled under the 1882 Edmunds Act, which banned plural marriages and gave U.S. marshals authority to arrest those who continued to practice polygamy.

Some or all of these factors may have played a part in the decision of a handful of local cattlemen to seize the army payroll as recompense for the financial, political, and religious hardships they were encountering.

Reenactment photo taken the day after the Wham Paymaster robbery.
Courtesy of the Arizona Historical Society/Tucson, AHS #44754

On May 8, 1889, Major Joseph Washington Wham set out from Tucson on his usual pay run. He had been an army paymaster for over ten years, handling innumerable payrolls for the military. He and his retinue stopped first at Fort Huachuca, then continued on to Fort Bowie. They spent the night in Willcox, where Wham picked up more funds waiting at the Willcox railroad depot, money necessary for the payrolls at Forts Grant, Thomas, and Apache, and Camp San Carlos.

A contingent of twelve buffalo soldiers from the 10th Cavalry and 24th Infantry at Fort Grant relieved Major Wham's initial escort, and he arrived at Fort Grant on May 10 without incident. Wham and his men started for Fort Thomas on Saturday morning, May 11, a run of about 45 miles. Major Wham's army ambulance led the way while the buffalo soldiers rode in a second wagon. The heavy oak strongbox in Major Wham's ambulance, marked "U.S. Treasury," contained $28,345.10 in gold and silver coins.

About 15 miles from Pima, the two wagons approached a hill descending into Cottonwood Wash, a dry and rocky arroyo. Major Wham's driver led the way, cautiously guiding his team of six mules down the steep hill. The soldiers lightened the load in the second wagon by getting out and walking. Just as the road narrowed, Major Wham's driver pulled to a sharp halt. In front of him, a massive boulder blocked his way.

Chances are it was Wilfred Webb and Mark Cunningham who boldly stood atop the bluff and aimed at the unsuspecting soldiers. As they began firing, Ed Follett rose up and shot the lead mule attached to the first wagon. Two more mules from the second wagon were dead within seconds. Chaos and bedlam took over the reins as the remaining burros reared and brayed, struggling to get out of harm's way. Caught in a web of tangled harnesses, the mules dragged the wagons, along with their dead companions, off the trail.

From atop the ridge a hailstorm of bullets rained down upon the military entourage. Some say Follett threw a handful of cartridges into a fire behind one of the boulders to give the illusion that hundreds of men were on the rim. The bandits freely scampered from one protective haven to the next, firing down on the small army at will. When one ducked for cover to reload, another popped up, sending a firestorm of lead careening down the hillside. The men seemed to enjoy their game of "cowboys versus cavalry," not even bothering to conceal their identities. One mistake they did make was believing the buffalo soldiers would not fight back. The bandits held the white man's belief that black soldiers would panic and run before they would fight.

The soldiers found little protection in the wash and returned fire as they sought refuge behind a low embankment. In less than an hour, Major Wham realized the futility of continuing the skirmish. Although no one was killed, only three soldiers remained unscathed. He ordered his men back beyond the line of fire.

The bandits giddily scurried down from their lofty perch to claim their ill-gotten fortune. They quickly cut the mules' tangled harnesses and chased them away, leaving the wounded soldiers stranded in the middle of the desert. Locating their prize, they hacked open the strongbox, grabbed the treasury bags, and fled.

Laughter rang out as the gunmen scattered. Tracks splayed across the desert with some leading directly toward local ranches, including the Follett ranch.

According to one newspaper report, more than 1,700 soldiers and Indian scouts set out in search of the payroll bandits. The trails confused the posses as some of the bandits reversed their horses' shoes, making it appear as if they were riding toward the robbery instead of away. In addition a band of wild horses had recently passed this way, leaving thousands of hoof prints.

The robbery was "without parallel in the history of crime in Arizona," reported the *Arizona Daily Citizen*. "Although seriously encumbered by the weight of money, they [the bandits] are evidently making rapid marches across the mountains, probably trying to get to Mexico."

Because this was a federal crime, U.S. Marshal William Kidder Meade, chief federal law officer in southern Arizona, headed the investigation. Federal agencies, as well as the governor of Arizona, offered numerous rewards for each man caught, enough incentive to round up a slew of suspects.

More than a dozen men were initially arrested and accused of taking part in the robbery. The *St. Johns Herald* protested that all the Mormons in Graham County had been apprehended. After the dust settled and a handful of men were released for lack of evidence, seven local cattlemen remained behind bars charged with the robbery of the army payroll.

Public opinion favored the defendants. They were seen as innocent farmers and ranchers who were being persecuted by an overbearing government. Some saw them as "Latter-Day Robin Hoods."

On September 20, 1889, the Arizona Territorial Court for the First Judicial District in Tucson convened. By October 2 they had handed down indictments against all seven defendants for robbing the army payroll. All entered pleas of "not guilty." The trial commenced on November 11.

Over a hundred witnesses were called, more than half testifying for the defense. Everyone had an alibi and a witness to back them up. As the *Arizona Journal-Miner* reported, "If the witnesses for the defense . . . are to be believed, it was a fellow named 'alibi' that robbed the paymaster last May."

The buffalo soldiers identified several of the defendants as the culprits who fired down from the barricades, but their testimony was tainted by the color of their skin. A black woman, Frankie Campbell, claimed she came upon the cattlemen as they were struggling to move the boulder onto the road. She said she witnessed the entire melee from behind the huge boulder, even sustaining bullet holes in her clothing. She identified most of the bandits by name.

One of the robbers lost a finger in the melee. Lyman Follett showed up in court missing a finger. Gilbert Webb, who was the only man able to pay his bail and remain free until trial, was accused of bribing witnesses. While out on bail, he paid off some of his debts in gold coins.

The air was filled with accusations and charges, bribery and falsehoods. Judges and lawyers came and went as each side accused the other of collusion and deceit, but on December 10, 1889, it was all over. The jurors were handed the case on December 14, and within two hours, including a lunch break, the jury of twelve free white men returned to the courtroom and acquitted the seven cattlemen of any wrongdoing. No one was ever convicted of robbing the army payroll.

Little changed in the tiny hamlet of Pima, Arizona Territory. Gilbert Webb lost his home over unpaid taxes, but he was eventually reinstated into the Mormon Church and served as a delegate to the Territorial Democratic Convention in 1890. Wilfred Webb, or W.T. as he was now called, entered politics serving as speaker of the Arizona House of Representatives and member of the Arizona Constitutional Convention.

His spread, the 76 Ranch, was eventually turned into a dude ranch.

Andy Carlson, the wide-eyed teenager who held the horses' reins as the robbery unfolded, remained a cowboy all his life.

The other acquitted men fell in and out with the law, but none ever admitted any part in the Wham payroll robbery.

Speculation still abounds as to whether the bulk of the army money may be stashed somewhere near the town of Pima, but in all probability, it is long gone.

Of the dozen buffalo soldiers who defended the army payroll, two were awarded the Medal of Honor and eight received commendations from the military.

Major Wham, initially charged with replacing the funds lost on his watch, eventually was released from of his financial burden by Congress.

In his later years, W.T. Webb was often asked if he had any part in the heist. His reply never wavered: "I neither confirm nor deny any involvement. To confirm would be to admit my guilt, but to deny would surely ruin a good story."

Augustine Chacón
Hombre Muy Malo

On the evening of December 18, 1895, Paul Becker, a clerk tending Mrs. McCormack's store in southern Arizona's Morenci Canyon, locked up and headed for the local saloon to grab a bite to eat. Three men watched him leave. Augustine Chacón, Pilar Franco, and Leonardo Morales climbed through a transom at the rear of the store looking for money, guns, and food—anything they could steal.

After Becker had his fill at the saloon, he headed back to McCormack's and walked in on the bandits. They ordered him to open the store safe. Becker lunged at the trio, knocking the gun out of one man's hand and grabbing for a knife held by another. The knife sliced across Becker's hand. They again demanded he open the safe and again Becker refused. According to Becker's later statement, Augustine Chacón then plunged a knife into the clerk's side and left him for dead. The three men left the way they came, richer by a mere $25 and two watches. Becker staggered back to the saloon where Constable Alex Davis removed the 6-inch knife still stuck in his side.

Augustine Chacón, a man who admitted to killing over fifty men during his lifetime, had struck fear around Morenci and across most of southern Arizona, long before he entered McCormack's store that night. And while his life did not start out on the wrong side of the law, he ended up on the wrong end of a hangman's noose.

Born in Sonora, Mexico, around 1856, Chacón claimed he worked as a farmhand and *vaquero* (cowboy), even hiring on for a while with the Mexican border patrol. Around 1888 he arrived in Morenci and was hired as a cowboy on Ben Ollney's ranch. Over 6 feet tall with a mass of

Augustine Chacón, "The Hairy One."
Courtesy of the Arizona Historical Society/Tucson, AHS #PC 161/F.5/I

black hair covering his body, including a voluminous beard and mustache, he aptly fit his nickname *El Peludo* or "The Hairy One."

Chacón earned the respect of his *compadres* on the ranch and his boss found no fault with his work until the day Chacón disputed the size of his paycheck and quit. Chacón and Ollney exchanged heated words, and at one point Ollney purportedly laughed in Chacón's face. Ollney drew his gun but was no match for the wily cowboy. When the smoke cleared, the rancher lay dying in the dust. Ranch hands raced to his rescue, but five cowboys also met their fate at the end of Chacón's gun.

Chacón hightailed it into the hills with a posse in hot pursuit. They quickly caught up with him; Chacón knew if he could not outrun a posse, he could certainly outshoot them. He killed four before a bullet smacked into his arm, yet he still managed to escape.

Chacón eluded the law for several months until someone recognized him one night near Fort Apache. He argued his innocence, but a vigilante group threw him in jail with the promise of a sunrise hanging.

When the first streaks of dawn peered between the barred windows of Chacón's cell, only a pile of hacksaw blades and a few sawed-off bars lay where the outlaw should have been sleeping. Some said Nelly Ollney, the rancher's daughter, who never believed Chacón murdered her father, provided the tools for his escape.

For the next few years, Chacón roamed back and forth across the Mexican border, earning his living by smuggling cattle and horses from one country to the other. He was back in Morenci by early 1894.

One cold winter morning, two clerks who worked at the nearby Detroit Copper Company made camp at Eagle Creek to enjoy a few days of hunting and fishing. When a band of outlaws came upon them, the naive young men stood no chance. The bandits were after guns and ammunition and lost little time eliminating the campers to acquire their goods. No one witnessed the killings, but Chacón was the name Morenci citizens put to the merciless slayings.

For a while Chacón hung around the town of Tombstone where outlaws and lawmen were often one and the same. It wasn't long before Cochise County Sheriff John Slaughter caught wind of Chacón's presence. Determined to bring him in, he and his deputy, Burt Alvord, found their man visiting friends in a large tent just outside of town. Alvord covered the front of the canvas building, Slaughter the back.

As Chacón fled out the back way, Slaughter fired, certain he had hit his man even though the night was as black as *El Peludo's* heart. Slaughter noticed one of the tent's guy ropes had broken and assumed Chacón had fallen over it, dying as he rolled down a ravine running behind the tent. With lanterns lighting the way, the lawmen headed down the abyss. But the ditch gave up no body. Chacón had apparently tethered his horse below for a quick getaway. Unscathed, he probably tripped over the rope just as Slaughter fired.

By now Chacón had few places he felt safe, but for some reason he kept returning to Morenci. Then came the break-in at McCormack's store.

The day after the robbery, Constable Davis, who was also a Graham County deputy sheriff, gathered a posse and followed the bandits' trail up a steep hill to a lowly cabin. From inside Chacón watched the posse approach. Suddenly, he bolted out the door, quickly followed by Franco and Morales. Gunfire exploded across the hillside as the bandits took refuge behind a barrier of huge boulders.

Eventually, Franco and Morales got to their horses and headed down the hill. Several of the posse followed, killing both men as they fled.

The war continued at the cabin. One member of the posse, Pablo Salcido, was a friend of Chacón's from their days as cowboys. Salcido convinced Davis he could talk Chacón into surrendering. He called to Chacón, and Chacón invited him to come ahead. As Salcido advanced, Chacón stepped into the open and fired one shot, felling his friend with a bullet through the head.

A hail of gunfire rained down upon the killer. Spent shells outnumbered the scraggly wildflowers scattered across the barren hillside in the bloodiest gunfight in Morenci's history.

Suddenly an eerie silence greeted the posse. Cautiously, they approached the boulder and found Chacón dazed with a bullet in his shoulder and a streak across his chest where another bullet had grazed him. Once again, *El Peludo* would be behind bars. But for how long?

Chacón recuperated in the Solomonville jail, a facility the *Arizona Republican* ridiculed as "the most insecure in the Territory." Charged with the murder of Pablo Salcido, he wasted no time proving the newspaper article correct when he casually walked out of his cell one evening. Crouching in a nearby ditch, he waited for a chance to flee out of town. His freedom was short-lived, however, when one of the men looking for him tripped and fell into the ditch on top of him.

On May 26, 1896, Chacón appeared before the Solomonville court and pled innocent to the killing of Pablo Salcido, claiming he would never shoot his friend. Despite his plea, he was convicted of murder and the hanging was set for July 24, 1896. To ensure he would still be around, he was sent to a more secure jail in Tucson until the date of his execution.

Chacón appealed his case to the Supreme Court of Arizona Territory, but the initial verdict was upheld. A group of citizens opposing the death penalty petitioned he serve life in the Yuma Territorial Prison, but they were also turned down. One newspaper claimed there was "a sentiment in Graham County amounting almost to a religious fervour against hanging [Chacón]." The delays extended his execution date to June 18, 1897. As he was being escorted back to Solomonville, he managed to saw off his shackles, but his escape attempt was quickly thwarted.

With only nine days to go before he faced the gallows, Chacón seemed destined, finally, to die. But The Hairy One had other ideas.

No one knew where he acquired his supply of tools, but visiting friends probably brought them in piece by piece. A band of sympathetic Mexican prisoners supposedly played guitars and sang a selection of loud, lively songs as he cut his shackles, burrowed into the thick adobe wall of his cell, and sawed through broad beams embedded in the stone walls. When he finally broke through, he tumbled into the sheriff's office and sailed out the window, once again a free man.

For the next five years, Chacón hid out on both sides of the border. More than one unsolved crime was blamed on him, and he probably did commit his share, such as the 1899 murder of two men found in their home near New River, their house ransacked and robbed by a group of marauders. The posse that trailed the culprits through Pinal County into Globe, then along the Black River, garnered a description of the men from the ranchers they passed. One of the desperadoes certainly fit Chacón's hairy countenance, but the killers were never caught.

In the late 1800s as the country expanded westward and territories attained statehood, Arizona Territory was repeatedly rejected in its bid for sovereignty. A major detriment facing Arizona was its reputation as a place where outlaws could still find refuge. In 1901 Territorial Governor Nathan Oakes Murphy organized the Arizona Rangers to enforce territorial law. Range boss Burton C. Mossman became the first captain of this new breed of lawmen and during his one-year term, he and his men eliminated some of the most notorious outlaw gangs in the territory. Mossman was determined to bring in Augustine Chacón before his term was up. By now Chacón only came into Arizona when he needed to sell off rustled Mexican cattle or horses.

In April 1902 Mossman recruited two lawmen-turned-outlaws to help him capture Chacón—ex-deputy constable Billy Stiles and Burt Alvord, the man who had once tried to capture Chacón with Sheriff Slaughter. Mossman promised leniency for the two scoundrels if they helped with his plot. They were to contact Chacón at his Mexican hide-out and entice him to cross the border into Arizona. Since Arizona

Rangers had no authority in Mexico, he needed to get Chacón into the U.S. before he could arrest him. Mossman posed as an escaped horse thief who desired some of rancher Colonel Bill Green's fine racehorses located just this side of the U.S.-Mexican border, but he wanted Chacón to sell the herd in Mexico. After sending the two reprobates into Mexico to contact Chacón, Mossman waited to see if the killer would take the bait. It was four months before he heard from his accomplices.

On August 31 Stiles met Mossman in the border town of Naco and handed the ranger a note from Alvord saying Chacón agreed to a meeting, "twenty-five miles within the Mexican line at the Socorro Mountain spring . . . ."

Mossman was not eager to cross into Mexico, well aware that if a Mexican patrol caught him arresting one of its citizens within its borders, he would be in deep trouble. But he was determined to get his man, so he and Stiles headed south. Three days later they met up with Chacón and Alvord.

Chacón was a reluctant host. His eyes never left the stranger who promised him good horseflesh. As Mossman, Alvord, and Stiles drank whiskey and exchanged small talk during the night, Chacón remained sober and silent. A drizzling rain left the men cold and uncomfortable, although Mossman had the protection of his yellow rain slicker. Beneath it his hand never left the hilt of his gun.

The next morning Mossman warmed himself by the fire. He pulled out a smoldering twig, bowed his head against the morning breeze, and breathed deeply to ignite his tightly rolled cigarette. He glanced over at Chacón, and there was no question in Mossman's mind who was in charge around this campfire. He willed himself to make no suspect moves that would anger his smoking partner. He had one chance to get the drop on Chacón. If he faltered, he would be dead before his cigarette hit the ground.

Alvord saddled his horse saying he would bring back fresh water. He had no intention of returning.

Wiping his brow, Mossman realized it was not the morning rain drizzling down his face but his own sweat. He knew he had to act now. In one swift motion, he dropped the burning twig into the fire, reached beneath his slicker, drew out his gun, and arrested one of the most notorious murderers in southern Arizona. The fact that the capture was illegal made no difference to Mossman at the moment. He ordered Stiles to disarm Chacón and handcuff him.

The three men rode out of camp with Stiles in the lead, holding the reins of Chacón's horse. Chacón traveled with a rope around his neck and his hands cuffed behind his back. Mossman brought up the rear as the outlaw parade made its way back into U.S. territory. Mossman watched his back for any signs of a Mexican patrol. His one-year commission as an Arizona Ranger had just expired.

Once in the U.S. Mossman flagged down a train heading into Benson for the final leg of the trip. Graham County Sheriff Jim Parks met the entourage with a new pair of handcuffs for Chacón and a set of leg irons.

A reporter on the train noted the haggard face of the forty-six-year-old bandit. "His form is bent and his beard is tinged with gray. To be hunted like a wild animal for five years has left its mark on the outlaw . . ." When asked where he was going, Chacón remarked, "I suppose they are taking me to Solomonville, and I want them to kill me this time. I prefer death to a term in the penitentiary." When the reporter asked Mossman where he had captured Chacón, Mossman replied, ". . . on a horse pasture located about seven miles this side of the Mexican line." Mossman and Sheriff Parks must have had a few moments to get their story straight because Parks backed up the lie.

Guards were posted outside the Solomonville jail, which had undergone a few changes since Chacón's last visit, including a new steel cage made just for him. However, the same gallows built in 1897 still waited, ensconced behind a 14-foot adobe wall to keep out the curious. Only those with invitations would be allowed to view the hanging.

The execution was scheduled for November 14, 1902, but once again, a citizens group petitioned to commute the sentence to life imprisonment, and once again, the argument was defeated. The date of the hanging was changed to November 21—Black Friday.

Chacón ate a hearty breakfast the morning of his execution, then visited with friends Sisto Molino and Jesus Bustos. He talked to the local Catholic priest several times during the day and finished off a big lunch. He put on a new black suit and shaved off his scraggly beard but left his drooping mustache intact. At 2:00 P.M. he headed toward the gallows.

As he entered the courtyard, about fifty people greeted him. Even more climbed nearby trees for a glimpse of *El Peludo*. He made his way up the steps of the gallows, passing the coffin that awaited him.

Chacón asked if he could have a cup of coffee and a cigarette before dying. He turned to the crowd and spoke to them in Spanish with an interpreter repeating his words. "It is nothing but right that when one is going to die that he be given a few moments of time to quietly smoke a cigarette."

For thirty minutes he rambled on, once again swearing his innocence in the shooting of Pablo Salcido. "I have a clean conscience," he said. Raising his right hand, he swore, "I am sure that this hand has never been guilty of murder. I may have stolen and done a good many other things, but I am innocent of this crime."

He asked for another cup of coffee, then sat down on the gallows steps to roll another cigarette and continue his conversation with the crowd. Finally, he was silent. "Is that all?" asked the interpreter. "*Si, es todo* (Yes, that's all)," Chacón replied.

Friends climbed the gallows steps to shake his hand. He asked to be allowed to live until 3:00 P.M., but his request was denied. "It's too late now," he said. "Time to hang." He was pronounced dead sixteen minutes later. Molino and Bustos carted off the body of their friend and buried him a few miles from Solomonville in San Jose.

The *Arizona Bulletin* reported the next day, "A nervier man than Augustine Chacón never walked to the gallows, and his hanging was a melodramatic spectacle that will never be forgotten by those who witnessed it."

Many years after Chacón's hanging, historian Ryder Ridgeway claimed he was giving a speech on outlaws in Oakland, California, when he noticed a stoic-looking man in the front row. The stranger showed little emotion as Ridgeway talked until he mentioned the name Augustine Chacón. Suddenly the man was consumed with emotion, tears streaming down his face. As Ridgeway concluded his speech, the man approached and bombarded him with questions about Chacón. Ridgeway asked what interest the stranger had in the old outlaw, and the man said he was Chacón's son. His mother had kept the truth of his father's reputation from him, saying he had died in Solomonville during a smallpox epidemic. Now he knew the truth.

In 1980 some of Chacón's family members dedicated a marble gravestone to the outlaw at the San Jose cemetery. On the marker, they inscribed the following words:

AUGUSTINE CHACÓN
HE LIVED LIFE
WITHOUT FEAR
HE FACED DEATH
WITHOUT FEAR
HOMBRE MUY BRAVO

Maybe he was *muy bravo* to some, but to most, he was the *hombre muy malo* (very bad man).

James Fleming Parker
"I Died Game and like a Man"

In the dwindling twilight, James Fleming Parker stumbled along the snow-slick trail of Diamond Creek Canyon near the foot of the majestic Grand Canyon. The chasm below held nothing but a deep abyss from which he would never return if his foot slipped on the treacherous path. The small caves that dotted the sheer walls held other terrors. Mountain lions and black bears made their homes along these steep parapets, and Parker certainly didn't want to spoil their sleep as he balanced gingerly on the precipice.

But what lay behind him was even more worrisome. A posse had been on his trail for days; he was exhausted and hungry. Traveling by foot since no horse could keep its footing on the rugged prominences, he had even walked through ice-encrusted waters to elude the persistent lawmen. As he crawled beneath a sheltering boulder, he dared not light a fire to warm his shivering, starving body. He found a flat stone and laid his head on the makeshift pillow. Parker knew he had made this cold, hard bed himself, and now he had to lie in it.

That snowy night in February 1897 was not the first time Parker had run afoul of the law. From his first breath in 1865, he was doomed to a life of hardship and trouble. At the age of fifteen, after his mother had died in childbirth and his father committed suicide, he was sentenced to California's San Quentin Penitentiary for stealing a steer.

Upon his release the teenager drifted into Arizona Territory and worked as a cowboy in the Prescott area. He became close friends with another ranch hand, George Ruffner, who would figure prominently in Parker's life.

Look Out for

Train Robber and Murderer.

$1000 REWARD

For the Arrest and Conviction of

FLEMING PARKER

Who escaped from County Jail at Prescott, Arizona, on or about May 13, 1897. In making his escape he shot and mortally wounded the Deputy District Attorney.

DESCRIPTION.

Fleming Parker, alias William Parker, is now about 31 years of age; 5 feet 7½ inches high; weighs 165 lbs.; light grey eyes; brown hair; size of foot 6½ inches; teeth in fair condition; high, full forehead; round features; straight nose; small mouth; round chin; vacine mark on left forearm; mole back of neck; scar on left side of head. Usually wears his hat on back of his head; is a cowboy by occupation, and a native of Tulare County. His picture as given hereon is a perfect likeness of him. He has served a term of five years in San Quentin for burglary. When last heard of he was heading for Nevada or Utah; had a repeating rifle with him. He was arrested for attempting to rob the A. & P. R. R. train at Peach Springs, Arizona, and was being held for trial in the Prescott Jail when he escaped. His partner Jim, alias Harry Williams of Utah, was killed at the time of the attempted robbery. There is no doubt of his conviction if captured. If arrested telegraph Sheriff Ruffner, Prescott, Arizona, or the undersigned.

J. N. THACKER,
SPECIAL OFFICER, WELLS, FARGO & CO.,
SAN FRANCISCO

SAN FRANCISCO, May 18, 1897.

Wanted poster distributed by Wells, Fargo & Co. for capture of Parker.

Sharlot Hall Museum Photo, Prescott, Arizona

Parker was an excellent wrangler. He and Ruffner participated in the July 4, 1888, Prescott rodeo, an event the town claims to be the first rodeo in history.

Parker never stayed in one place long. He returned to California and once again landed in San Quentin for stealing a farmer's wheat supply. Originally sentenced to five years, he was released on a technicality after serving only nine months.

By 1895 he was back in Arizona working for Charlie "Hog-Eye" Miller at the Hat Ranch near Williams, Arizona, a town comprised of lean-to shacks, one church, and about thirty saloons.

Parker had been at the Hat Ranch just a few months when horses and cattle began disappearing around northern Arizona at an alarming rate. A breeder who hired Parker to break a band of wild horses soon discovered several of his herd missing, but he did not initially suspect the good-looking, personable young man. However, after Parker started hanging out with Abe Thompson and his gang, known cattle and horse rustlers, the breeder suspected his hired hand of instigating the theft.

Abe Thompson and his men roamed northern Arizona pilfering cattle and horses, then driving them to market in southern Nevada. When more than forty horses turned up missing from a loading pen near Seligman, Thompson's gang was immediately suspected of the heist. And although a posse caught two of the rustlers, the rest of the gang escaped, riding into their almost unapproachable hideout in Robber's Roost, a canyon surrounded by towering walls and treacherous trails that lay near the confluence of Diamond Creek with the Colorado River.

Parker continued to remain relatively free of the law even though his name was often associated with missing livestock. In 1896 he went to work for Tom Wagner on the Bar Cross Ranch, near Williams, and had an opportunity to show his more compassionate side when Wagner got caught between a calf he had roped to brand and its irate mother. As the bovine took off after him and with only one direction to run, Wagner was heading straight toward a cliff when Parker rode up and lassoed the cow, saving Wagner from certain death.

Parker eventually became the undisputed leader of the Thompson gang. He preferred rustling horses over cattle, as they were easier to move about and didn't complain as loudly. But he was looking for even more excitement and much more money.

Trains had been running through Prescott since 1887 carrying gold bullion out of California to wealthy eastern investors. Parker had no love of locomotion, particularly after a train hit two of his own horses and he received a mere pittance from the railroad for his loss. He decided to hit up one of the trains to get his fair settlement. He was not at all concerned about an 1888 law that made train robbery a capital offense punishable by hanging.

He set about determining when gold was scheduled to be shipped through Arizona on the Atlantic & Pacific Railroad and soon learned that a healthy amount of bullion would be transported on the eastbound train on February 8, 1897. The train would have to slow almost to a crawl as it struggled up a steep grade and maneuvered a sharp curve at Rock Cut, about halfway between Peach Springs and Nelson, small whistle stops along Arizona's northern frontier.

Parker rode into Peach Springs, sold his horse, and bought a one-way ticket to Barstow, telling everyone he had obtained work in California. When he climbed aboard the westbound train, he carried only his saddle, a bedroll, and his guns.

As the train pulled into Barstow, Parker got off, turned around, and boarded an eastbound commuter for southern Nevada. From there he acquired a horse and made his way back into Arizona. He took only one accomplice with him as he headed for Rock Cut, a man named Williams or Wilson whose true identity was never known.

On the night of February 8, the two men tethered their horses behind a small thicket along the tracks, the fire from copious cigarettes their only warmth. As the train slowed at the curve, Parker grabbed the ladder, jumped aboard the locomotive, leveled his gun on the engineer and fireman, and ordered them to stop the train. His partner was to uncouple the engine and express car, then fire two shots alerting Parker to move the two cars away from the rest of the train. They would unload the gold from the express car and be on their way. When Parker heard the signal, he commanded the engineer to move the locomotive and second car a few miles down the tracks.

He tied up the engineer and fireman and climbed into what he thought was the express car. On this train, however, the mail car had been coupled to the locomotive instead of the expected express car loaded with gold. Parker made the best of the situation and rifled through the mail looking for anything of value. He got away with about $5.

When the train made its unexpected stop, the Wells, Fargo agent and mail clerk knew something was up. With guns drawn, they cautiously made their way to the front of the train where they spotted the second outlaw uncoupling the cars. The two shots Parker heard were those that killed his accomplice.

When his colleague failed to appear, Parker untied the engineer and fireman and instructed them to take the locomotive back down the track, couple the cars together, and get out of there. He watched as the train passed by and stayed nearby until morning. But at dawn's light, the only sign of his partner was blood on the tracks. Parker took off for Robber's Roost.

When the robbery was reported in Peach Springs, George Ruffner, who was now the Yavapai County sheriff, along with Coconino County Sheriff Ralph Cameron and Mohave County Sheriff Bill Lake, plus a handful of deputies and Indian trackers, took up the search for the lone train robber.

For days the posse stayed close on Parker's trail, even following the circles he rode in to confuse them. But the trail became more rigorous and the temperature quickly dropped below freezing. When fresh snow obliterated all traces of Parker's whereabouts, the posse finally quit. Parker watched the men ride out of the canyon back to town.

The outlaw was also suffering from the elements, however. To keep his feet from freezing, he walked rather than rode his horse. At some point he removed his boots and wrapped clothing around his feet, maybe after fording Diamond Creek. He slept in caves with rocks as his pillow. Yet as cold as he was, he believed he had escaped unscathed.

On February 22, back on the trail with fresh horses, the posse camped in a side canyon that emptied into Diamond Creek. A couple of deputies scouring for firewood came upon a tethered horse, its hoof prints matching those they had been following. One of the men stayed behind while the other reported back to camp. Soon a whistling Parker came strolling up the creek bed, his Winchester casually draped across his shoulder. The deputy wasted no time making his presence, and his rifle, known to the train robber. The outlaw gave up without incident.

Parker was incarcerated in Prescott and charged with train robbery. He shared a cell with accused forger Lewis C. Miller and Cornelia Sarata (sometimes spelled Asarta), arrested for assault. As always, however, Parker soon tired of his surroundings and desired a new location. On May 9, 1897, he escaped. If he had stayed in jail, he might have received a fairly light sentence since his bounty from the train robbery was so small, but when he made his bid for freedom, things did not go well.

The warm spring day afforded no breeze through the stifling jail. The prisoners demanded water. Jailer Robert Meador allowed Sarata, a trustee, to fetch a couple of buckets to quench their thirsts. Returning with full water buckets, Sarata stood behind Meador as the jailer unlocked the cell door. Parker rammed the door into Meador's face. Sarata wrestled him to the ground as Parker grabbed the heavy ring of jail keys and slugged Meador over the head.

Parker ran into the next room and grabbed a handful of weapons. He was almost to the front door when Assistant County Attorney Lee

Norris, hearing Meador's cries, dashed down the stairs to see what all the ruckus was about. As soon as he saw Parker, Norris turned in retreat, but Parker had no intention of letting the attorney sound an alarm. The bullet hit Norris square in the back. He lingered through the night but died before dawn. Norris had just asked his sweetheart to marry him.

Parker, Sarata, and Miller raced to a livery stable across from the jail. Parker was a connoisseur of good horseflesh, having once proclaimed, "They'll hang you just as high for stealin' a sorry hoss as for the best." He needed only an instant to spot the finest horse in the stable, a pure white beauty considered the fastest steed in the territory. Sure-Shot belonged to his old pal Sheriff Ruffner. As Parker jumped aboard Sure-Shot, Miller and Sarata grabbed one horse and rode double as the trio hightailed it out of town.

About 150 men set out after the escaped prisoners. Ruffner, who was out of town when the jailbreak occurred, caught up with the posse at Lynx Creek where they had cornered the three desperadoes. Shots rang out as the two sides squared off. Miller suddenly fell off the horse he shared with Sarata. As the threesome fled, Parker plucked Miller off the ground and onto Sure-Shot.

Some sources claim Jailer Meador fired three shots as the men fled their cells, one bullet hitting Sarata. Others believe Sarata was wounded at Lynx Creek. Whatever shape he was in, as Miller climbed aboard Sure-Shot, Sarata rode off, never to be seen again.

Parker and Miller fled across the valley with the posse and a team of bloodhounds in hot pursuit. Eventually, the two men parted ways with Miller, who was on foot, heading toward Jerome and nursing a wound he received either at the hands of Jailer Meador or at the Lynx Creek skirmish. Nine days later, he gave himself up. Parker, however, was in no mood to return to the Prescott jail.

"Parker, the train robber and murderer, with a pack of bloodhounds and officers of the law on his trail, has baffled his pursuers and no doubt is safe from pursuit in the wilds of a country no one is more familiar with than he," bemoaned one May 16 newspaper article. ". . . the fox is smarter than the hounds."

Parker made good time heading back to Robber's Roost, his old haunt. Sheriff Ruffner, however, was determined not to let the horse thief get away, particularly on his prize mount. He put up $1,000 of his own money for Parker's capture, bringing the total on the outlaw's head to $4,000. The two men, who knew each other so well from their days as cowboys, stayed almost within shooting distance of each other, but Parker knew the terrain better and continually eluded his adversary.

He even had time for a little tomfoolery. Ruffner came across a piece of paper Parker had placed conspicuously on the trail. "A reward of $1,000 is offered by the undersigned for Sheriff Ruffner dead or alive," the note read, "—dead preferred."

Parker hid out with a band of sheepmen who obliterated his tracks by herding their flock across his path. The sheepmen had no use for lawmen who often gave them trouble.

As he made his way toward Robber's Roost, Parker happened upon an empty ranch house. He took time to reshoe Sure-Shot, but put the horse's shoes on backwards, then rode along a river bottom for several miles to confuse the posse before replacing Sure-Shot's shoes properly.

Tom Wagner, the man who owed his life to Parker, found one of his best horses missing one day, but in its place stood a very tuckered-out Sure-Shot. With his proclivity for good horseflesh, Parker soon abandoned Wagner's horse but acquired another from a livery stable in Williams.

Parker's trail eventually led to Hog-Eye Miller's Ranch, a place he was still welcome. When the bloodhounds picked up his scent, he headed into the Bill Williams Mountains, a tough ride for any man, horse, or dog over jagged granite rocks and loose shale. The hounds' paws were soon torn and bleeding as they scrambled through the rough terrain, forcing the posse to return to town.

The next morning, sporting booties on their feet, the dogs picked up the scent again, but within a short time they began sneezing and howling. Parker had sprinkled pepper along the trail.

On May 23 two Navajo Indians spotted Parker camping near the Little Colorado River and reported their discovery to Samuel S. Preston, proprietor of a local trading post. Preston notified Sheriff Cameron in Flagstaff who immediately telegraphed Ruffner in Prescott.

Not waiting for Ruffner to join them, Preston, Cameron, and about ten Navajo trackers headed out to find their prey. Just before daylight on May 26, the posse crept into Parker's camp as his fire smoldered and his horse snorted nervously in the predawn air. When one of the Indians fired a shot, Parker awoke with a start, a dozen guns aimed at his head.

With the outlaw in tow, the men started for Flagstaff, camping for the night near the Little Colorado River. Never one to give up when the odds looked decidedly against him, Parker strategized he would grab one of the tracker's guns and escape into the surrounding heavy brush. He was just about to make his move when Ruffner rode into camp to join the posse. Parker knew he stood no chance of eluding his old buddy.

Parker was placed in the Flagstaff jail where Lewis Miller was already occupying a cell. Not willing to take his eyes off his nemesis, Ruffner spent the night on a cot outside Parker's cell.

The next morning, with shackles on their feet, Parker and Miller hobbled their way to the train station for the ride into Prescott.

Just outside the tiny town of Whipple, the train made an unscheduled stop and Ruffner hustled the two outlaws off the train and into a waiting wagon. He had been warned that a lynch mob was forming at the Prescott depot and ordered his prisoners to be taken directly to the courthouse, determined they would arrive with their heads intact.

Ruffner's information was not quite accurate. About 200 men were waiting in Prescott, but they were at the courthouse, not the train station. When Ruffner pulled up, Miller panicked. "My God, they're coming to hang us," he cried. But Parker was more philosophical. "Try to have a little courage," he told Miller. "They can only hang you once." Ruffner, with his twin-barreled shotgun loaded and aimed, stoically told the crowd to go home.

On June 15, 1897, Parker was tried for the murder of Lee Norris. It took only three days to find him guilty. He was never charged with the train robbery.

Miller was given a life sentence as an accessory in Norris's murder. He served ten years in Yuma Territorial Prison and was released.

Parker's hanging was scheduled for Friday, August 13, but legal delays and appeals postponed the execution until June 3, 1898.

Supposedly acquiring religion while awaiting his fate, Parker was baptized into the Catholic faith just days before his hanging. But on the eve of his last day on earth, when Ruffner asked if he had any last requests, the condemned man purportedly requested a visit from Flossie, one of the girls on Whiskey Row.

The morning of the hanging, Ruffner read Parker the death warrant and escorted him to the scaffold. Given the chance to speak, Parker replied, "I claim that I am getting something that ain't due me, but I guess every man who is about to be hanged says the same thing, so that don't cut no figure; whenever the people says I must go, I am one who can go and make no kick."

As the black hood was placed over his head, he asked it be removed so he could shake hands with everyone on the scaffold. When he got to the jailer, he gave him a message for the other prisoners. "[T]ell the boys that I died game and like a man." He requested his old friend, George Ruffner, replace the hood. As he did so, Ruffner sprang the trap that sent Parker to his death.

James Fleming Parker was taken to potter's field for burial. Sheriff George Ruffner drove the hearse.

Albert Wright
"Burt" Alvord
—————— ·»•·«· ——————
Bandit with a Badge

O n the evening of September 9, 1899, Willcox, Arizona, Constable
Burt Alvord, who was also a deputy sheriff for Cochise County,
surveyed the poker hand in front of him and ordered another
round of drinks at Schwertner's Saloon. He enjoyed hanging out with
Willcox's local boys, even if the cards in front of him were not profitable
tonight. His pleasant evening was suddenly disrupted when a messenger
burst through the saloon door—bandits had robbed the Southern Pacific
train at Cochise Station! Alvord jumped up, his 6-foot frame towering above
the gathering crowd. Visibly upset that someone had moved in on his territory, he immediately rounded up a posse and headed to the crime scene.

His two deputies, Billy Stiles and Bill Downing, joined the posse at
Cochise Station. He ordered Stiles to take some men and head north
and Downing to take the southern route. Alvord led a third group
toward the Chiracahua Mountains. The bandits had been clever though.
They had followed a rock-hard riverbed, exhausted of rain for months,
leaving few hoof prints to follow. Alvord finally ordered the men back to
town without finding any trace of the robbers.

Speculation grew as to who could have masterminded such a successful robbery. Almost a year passed before Willcox's own constable, the tall,
sometimes ruthless but fun-loving Albert Wright "Burt" Alvord was fingered as ringleader of a group of men who straddled both sides of the law.

Alvord certainly started out on the right side of justice. His father,
after bringing the family from California to Tombstone in 1880, often

Albert Wright "Burt" Alvord, circa 1897.
Courtesy of the Arizona Historical Society/Tucson, AHS #13878

served as the town's justice of the peace. Born Albert Wright Alvord in Susanville, California, on September 11, 1867, Burt was a young teen when he arrived in Tombstone. He may have witnessed the O.K. Corral gunfight on October 26, 1881. He sometimes worked at the corral, sweeping out stables, tending horses, and making repairs.

Burt received most of his education on the streets of Tombstone. He could shoot billiards with the best of the cowboys, and his whittling was of expert quality. He loved to play practical jokes and often resolved differences from his pranks with his fists, sometimes a gun. He particularly enjoyed a good bar fight.

In 1886 Cochise County Sheriff John H. Slaughter enlisted Alvord as deputy sheriff. Slaughter knew the twenty-year-old could handle himself with a gun and often acted on instinct. Frequently, the two lawmen surprised sleeping bandits by shucking their boots before sneaking into enemy camps. Although careful to note that they warned suspected culprits to surrender before firing and insisting the men almost always reached for their guns, Slaughter and Alvord brought in few live prisoners.

Alvord earned a reputation as a hard-riding, quick-shooting lawman. He took part in such notable events as the search for suspects in the 1889 Wham Paymaster Robbery and the attempted capture of notorious killer Augustine Chacón, one of the most feared desperadoes in Arizona Territory.

Alvord discovered that hunting down outlaws sometimes brought lucrative profits. After killing a horse thief, he confiscated the bandit's cartridge/money belt, including $500 in gold. Sometimes he rode with another illegal equine collector, Eduardo Lopez, stealing Papago ponies and selling them for about $10 each. Sheriff Slaughter usually ignored his deputy's indiscretions.

Alvord served as deputy to several sheriffs after John Slaughter. "He was not one to mess with," according to historian Don Chaput, "but good to have around if force was a consideration." He knew the surrounding terrain as well as he knew how much whiskey was behind the bar. If things got out of hand during one of his practical jokes, the sheriff at the time was inclined to look the other way and let him have his fun.

He almost got himself killed in 1890 when he and Biddy Doyle played one prank too close to the vest. After fixing a wrestling match, the two men hightailed it out of Bisbee with the money purse and an angry mob close behind. Another time, he and Max Marks, after enjoying a lengthy session at a Bisbee saloon, telegraphed the *Tombstone Epitaph* that the "bodies of Marks and Alvord will arrive this afternoon." Two coffins waited in somber silence outside the O.K. Corral stage stop. As passengers departed the stage, so did Alvord and Marks. "Sure our bodies arrived," they said. "We never go out without 'em."

In 1894 gold was discovered in the tiny town of Pearce, about 20 miles east of Tombstone. With the mines came saloons, dance halls, and unruly miners hell-bent on having a good time. In 1896 Alvord became deputy constable of Pearce, and before long the little community was as peaceful as a cow pasture. He married Lola Ochoa and bought a house in town and a ranch in the Dragoon Mountains. Maybe his days of straddling both sides of the law were behind him.

Alvord's reputation for cleaning up towns spread. In June 1897 he was asked to take on the job of deputy constable at Willcox. A month later Willcox's constable resigned, and Alvord took over the position.

While Pearce's problems stemmed from celebrating miners, Willcox entertained tough-riding cowboys. On one occasion a bunch of Friday-night buckaroos caught Alvord and his deputies off guard at Kasper Hauser's saloon. As they locked the lawmen in the basement, the entertainment started upstairs.

The next morning Cowboy Billy King let Alvord out and apologized for his part in the prank. King even offered to buy Alvord a new hat since his was demolished in the night's revelry. Alvord rubbed his shiny bald head, and, although somewhat aggravated that the joke was on him this time, he slapped King on the back and escorted him out the saloon door. Shots rang out. Alvord returned to the saloon alone, gun in hand, claiming he killed King in self-defense. No charges were filed against Willcox's tough new constable.

In early 1899 Cochise County Sheriff Scott White again made Alvord a deputy. Between his constable job in Willcox and his job as Cochise County deputy sheriff, Alvord enjoyed authority across most of southeastern Arizona and acquired as many enemies as he did friends. To protect his back, he made Billy Stiles his deputy in Willcox, and sometimes enlisted the help of Bill Downing, a man of questionable background, and Matt Burts, a barfly.

Alvord managed Willcox so well, he was spending more of his time in local saloons than hunting down outlaws. With little money to spend (lawmen made paltry salaries), he devised the scheme to rob the Southern Pacific train at Cochise Station.

Alvord figured the payroll for the Pearce mines should be on board the westbound Southern Pacific train the night of September 9, 1899. He knew the engine had to slow to a crawl as it climbed the steep grade outside Cochise Station, just a few miles from Willcox. It was the perfect spot for a holdup. He had no trouble convincing his three deputies—Stiles, Downing, and Burts—to perform the heist.

Alvord and his deputies broke into a local mercantile to obtain the dynamite they needed. They struck a nearby mining camp to stock up on explosive caps and fuses. Downing supplied the horses. They were ready.

The train ascended the hill and let out one final exhaustive sigh of steam as it came to a stop beneath the water tank. As Engineer C.A. Richardson readied the powerful machine to take on nourishment, he was suddenly facing the wrong end of a six-gun. Burts ordered Richardson and the fireman to uncouple the engine and move the mail and express cars away from the rest of the train toward a cluster of desert brush. Stiles disarmed the mail clerk and Wells, Fargo agent.

Down the track Downing emerged from the bushes and ordered Richardson to take the engine several hundred yards away from the mail and express cars. The three amigos placed a thundering amount of dynamite in the two cars. They set the charge and ducked for cover. The cars exploded hundreds of feet in the air with cash, gold coins, and jewelry blowing across the desert, creating a bountiful rainfall of wealth. The bandits quickly gathered the loot, jumped on horses secreted in the brush, and rode hard for parts unknown.

Meanwhile, Burt Alvord played poker in the Willcox saloon.

Even today, no one agrees how much money and gold was on the train; some figures ran as high as $80,000. Since the Pearce payroll was on an earlier train, chances are the men realized much less than they anticipated. It was later determined that Alvord distributed a small portion of the loot to his accomplices, but most of it was never found.

Feeling flush with his first victory, Alvord struck again. This time, the scheme was a little more complicated, but the stakes were just as lucrative. As before, he would take no role in the actual robbery, showing himself around town while the action happened far from his presence.

There were a few glitches.

Alvord enlisted Stiles to waylay Wells, Fargo agent Jeff Milton in Nogales. He did not want Milton on board the targeted train out of Nogales to Benson. Milton was a crack shot, and no savvy outlaw dared challenge him. At the last minute, however, Milton was called to replace the scheduled agent. He forgot to tell Stiles who was waiting for him in Nogales.

The night of February 14, 1900, was as dark as a gunslinger's soul. Five men huddled against the cold deep in the Dragoon Mountains. Three of them, Bob Brown and brothers George and Lewis Owens, were ranch hands. Bravo Juan Yoas and Three-Fingered Jack Dunlap already had accumulated criminal records. Only the promise of a train full of gold kept the men warm.

Burt Alvord was at his usual post—lining up drinks at a Benson saloon.

On the morning of February 15, the New Mexico & Arizona train left Nogales as scheduled, except for the presence of Jeff Milton instead of the regular Wells, Fargo agent. It made one scheduled stop in Fairbank, about 20 miles south of Benson, arriving near sundown. As passengers filled the platform, no one noticed the five men mingling with the crowd.

The Brown brothers entered the engine's cab without incident, disarming the engineer and fireman.

When Jeff Milton opened the express car doors, no one was more surprised to see him than the three desperadoes who had made their way to the front of the crowd. But with little hesitation, they demanded Milton drop his weapons. Milton hesitated to shoot into the crowd until one of the bandits fired a shot through the agent's hat. In one quick move, Milton grabbed his rifle and opened fire.

The bandits blasted the rail car, wounding Milton as they boarded. They searched frantically for the keys to the safe. Milton, barely conscious, managed to grab his shotgun and hit Dunlap full force; some of the buckshot ended up in Yoas's rump.

Aware the gunfight had aroused more attention than they could handle and with no luck finding the keys to the safe, the men dragged the mortally wounded Dunlap off the train, grabbed their horses, and fled, richer by less than $50. They split up as they ran, abandoning Dunlap by the side of the road.

The next day the posse found Dunlap next to a blackened cactus. He had tried to start a fire but only succeeded in burning the plant as well as himself. The dying man survived the trip to Tombstone and lived a few more days, plenty of time to finger the culprits in the Fairbank heist, including the two who were nowhere near the robbery site—Burt Alvord and Billy Stiles. Dunlap also told all he knew about the Cochise Station robbery, again naming Alvord as the leader and implicating Stiles, Matt Burts, and Bill Downing.

The suspects were rounded up and jailed in Tombstone's tiny facility. Only Stiles remained free after he sang loud and fast to authorities about his part in the two robberies and named Alvord as ringleader. Alvord vehemently denied his involvement in both incidents. He did not relish sitting in a jailhouse with criminals he had arrested, and he had no intention of staying there.

On April 8 Stiles walked into the jailhouse and asked to speak to Alvord. Afterwards, as the jailer led Alvord back to his cell, Stiles stuck a gun in the officer's side and relieved him of the jail keys. Alvord unlocked the cell doors, but only Bravo Juan Yoas walked out—the rest chose to take their chances at trial. Grabbing guns and rifles, the trio headed for the door, but the jailer made one last attempt to stop them. Stiles shot him in the leg as they fled.

About a week later Sheriff Scott White received a package in the mail. In it were the keys to the Tombstone jail and a note from the three escapees: "Tell the boys we are all well and eating regular." Alvord treated the whole episode as another of his pranks.

For three months the men were on the run. Stiles finally headed to his home in Casa Grande, leaving the other two riding toward Mexico. During their stay south of the border, Alvord and Yoas may have worked as armed guards in Mexican mines, since Alvord was as fluent in Spanish as was Yoas.

In 1902 Arizona Ranger Captain Burton C. Mossman set out to capture the killer Augustine Chacón and needed Alvord's help to bring in the desperado. Alvord may have ridden with Chacón at one time and the killer trusted him. When Alvord met up with Mossman in Mexico, he had been on the run for two years and was nursing a broken wrist. Mossman promised to recommend a lighter sentence for Alvord if he helped capture Chacón.

Alvord was ready to return to the states and once he put Mossman in touch with Chacón, he fled north. A week later, Alvord surrendered to Sheriff Del Lewis in the border town of Naco.

On December 1, 1902, Alvord appeared before a Tombstone judge. His attorney argued that Bill Downing had been found not guilty of the train heist because a jury thought the mandatory death penalty too harsh a judgment for robbing a train. The court agreed and ordered charges against Alvord dismissed.

Other allegations still loomed however—the jailbreak and wounding of the Tombstone jailer, plus far more serious federal charges of tampering with the U.S. mail during the Cochise Station robbery. By December 8 Alvord was back in jail but paid his bail and walked out after serving eight days.

In July 1903 a Grand Jury indicted Alvord on six counts of tampering with the U.S. mail. Bail was set at $9,000. This time, the man who had initiated the robbery of two money-laden trains had no hard cash to pay for his release.

Stiles fled rather than testify against Alvord but was recaptured. Not wanting the two desperadoes in the same jail, authorities sent Alvord to Phoenix to await trial while Stiles hung out in a Tucson facility. Both men were transported to Tombstone a few days before their December 10 trial date.

Unexpectedly, Alvord withdrew his "not guilty" plea and pled "guilty" to robbing the U.S. mail. The court dismissed five additional charges against him, reducing his sentence to two years in the Yuma Territorial Prison.

While Alvord waited to be transported to Yuma, he languished in the aging Tombstone jail with his old pal Stiles. The men wasted no time letting themselves out.

On the evening of December 15, Alvord and Stiles slithered through a hole they had dug in the jail's adobe wall and walked away.

After stealing a couple of horses, they made one stop before heading toward the border. With their horses hidden behind a dry goods store and their guns drawn, the two escapees rapped on the shop's back door. Young Percy Bowden, who would later become a lawman, "opened the door to find two men with guns drawn and pointing in my direction." The men ordered Bowden to bring them warm clothes and supplies. After hearing all the chores the boy did each day—milking sixteen cows and delivering the milk before school, sweeping the store, and cleaning windows—they suggested their line of work was more lucrative but "might not last as long if the law caught up with them . . ." They handed Bowden two $20 gold pieces and disappeared into the night.

By January 1904 a $500 reward hung over each man's head. Accused of several robberies in the Sonora area, Alvord later claimed he had nothing to do with any of them. One of these thefts included $8,000 in gold bullion that was never recovered.

On February 19 Alvord and Stiles were spotted hanging out at a ranch west of Naco, Sonora. Arizona Rangers surprised the two outlaws, severely wounding Alvord. Stiles escaped.

On March 3 Alvord entered Yuma Territorial Prison. He was released sometime around October 3, 1905. For a time, he lived with his sister in Los Angeles, then disappeared. Many believe he ended up on the Caribbean island of Barbados, changed his name to Tom Wright, and died of fever in 1910. At the time, he had in his possession about $800 in gold, which was released to his sister.

In 1938 two of Alvord's nieces filed a note with the Arizona Historical Society stating their uncle had died on a small island off the Atlantic coast of Panama, "about the Fall of 1910."

Burt Alvord turned his back on justice, discarding his badge for a robber's six-gun. As one of Arizona Territory's most notorious bad men, he is remembered more for his lawlessness than his success in bringing justice to a handful of unruly western towns.

——⟶•◀— Pearl Hart ——⟶•◀—
Pearl of the West

Henry Bacon whistled to keep himself company as he drove the stagecoach along the Globe road toward Florence, a distance of about 60 miles:

> The sun was brightly shining on a pleasant afternoon
> My partner speaking lightly said, "The stage will be here soon."
> We saw it coming around the bend and called to them to halt,
> And to their pockets we attended, if they got hurt it was their fault.

The May breeze blew warmly across his face and brought back memories of days when he was one of many stagecoach drivers traveling across the stark Arizona desert. Now, he chauffeured one of the last stage routes in existence and there was none of the old excitement in the journey.

He missed the camaraderie of a sidekick shotgun rider who watched for dastardly robbers waiting in ambush. Stagecoaches used to carry gold-laden strongboxes and packages of registered mail filled with lucrative stashes of cash and jewelry. With the expansion of railroads across the nation, most gold shipments these days traveled by train, and he couldn't remember the last time he had heard of a stagecoach robbery.

His three passengers nodded off as the afternoon sun permeated the coach. Slowing to maneuver the curve near Cane Springs Canyon, Bacon spotted a couple of cowboys hailing him to stop. "Probably need a lift," he thought. "Might as well pick 'em up. Got plenty of room and no strongbox on board."

As he reined in the horses, the two strangers suddenly pulled pistols and aimed directly at Bacon. They ordered his hands up and relieved him of his Colt .45 revolver, then pulled the passengers out of the coach.

Pearl Hart

They were an odd pair, Bacon thought as he steadied the horses. The one leveling a gun at his chest sported a shock of dark hair dangling from a scrunched-down hat and looked to be in his mid-twenties. And while this man seemed perfectly capable of shooting anyone who disagreed with him, it was the other bandit that drew Bacon's attention.

The second robber was particularly small, and at first Bacon thought he might be a young boy, maybe about fifteen years old. But as he looked closer, he realized that the soft gray eyes peering from beneath the overly large white sombrero, and the easily identifiable bosom underneath the gray flannel shirt belonged to a woman. As she blistered off an alphabet of cussedness, she rifled through the passengers' pockets and came up with around $400.

> While the birds were sweetly swinging, and the men stood up in line
> And the silver softly ringing as it touched this palm of mine.
> There we took their money, but left them enough to eat
> And the men looked so funny as they vaulted to their seats.

The lady bandit searched inside the coach and retrieved two guns. ". . . I can't see why men carry revolvers," she would later muse, "because they almost invariably give them up at the very time they were made to be used."

Bacon also carried a few dollars and the two robbers let him keep his money, but the woman tucked the driver's revolver into her waistband. The bandits gallantly returned $1 to each passenger to pay for grub when they arrived in town.

Ordering the passengers back into the coach, the outlaws turned and fled into the hills.

> Then up the road we galloped, quickly through a canyon we did pass
> Over the mountains we went swiftly, trying to find our horses grass,
> Past the station we boldly went, now along the riverside,
> And our horses being spent, of course we had to hide.

Bacon whipped his horses into a frenzy and hightailed it back to Globe to report the robbery. As soon as Pinal County Sheriff William E. Truman was notified, he formed a posse and set out after the culprits. Truman was pretty sure he knew the outlaws. Joe Boot, a downtrodden miner and jack-of-all-trades, had been seen in the area recently with Pearl Hart, a woman of questionable character.

The chase lasted just a few days, since the two bandits left a trail even a tenderfoot could follow. Seeming to have no plan of escape, Joe and Pearl drifted through the towns of Riverside and Mammoth. They slept by day and traveled at night, stole food for themselves and hay for their horses, and got thoroughly drenched when torrential rains hit the area. One day, they crawled into a cave for shelter and met up with an angry musk hog that Joe shot.

> In the night we would travel, in the daytime try and rest,
> And throw ourselves on the gravel, to sleep we would try our best.
> Around us our horses were stamping, looking for some hay or grain,
> On the road the Posse was tramping, looking for us all in vain.

Four days after the daring daylight robbery, Sheriff Truman walked up to the pair sleeping on the rain-soaked ground, grabbed their weapons, nudged them awake with the toe of his boot, and arrested them for robbing the stagecoach. Joe placidly surrendered but Pearl let out a torrent of expletives damning first the sheriff and then Joe for not putting up a fight. Truman was grateful the lady wildcat could not reach her gun. "She would have killed me in my tracks could she had got to her pistol," he said a few days later. "Surely women are curious creatures."

> One more day they would not have got us, but my horse got sore
>   and thin,
> And my partner was a mean cuss, so Billy Truman roped us in.
> Thirty years my partner got, I was given five,
> He seemed contented with his lot, and I am still alive.

According to the *Arizona Sentinel*, Pearl Taylor Hart wrote this poem while languishing in her Yuma Territorial Prison cell after being sentenced to serve five years, not for robbing the Globe stagecoach on May 29, 1899, but for taking the Colt .45 from driver Henry Bacon. While her poetic expression lacked any balance of symmetry or syntax, her creative endeavor played across the country's newspapers as another chapter in Pearl's already checkered and often fictional history. She memorialized her famous stage robbery in these lines and relished the fame, albeit no fortune, that followed.

Many of the facts about Pearl Hart are skewed by her own vivid imagination. Once she tasted the thrill of celebrity, she continually elaborated on her stage-robbing escapade. Journalists picked up every tale she told and many accepted her utterances as the gospel truth.

Over time historians have pieced together some of the facts of Pearl Hart's life, but since she freely twisted her history to suit an immediate situation, some truths may never be known. And although there are those who believe the lady outlaw was an ignorant morphine addict and harlot, in reality, she was a high-energy, educated young woman who happened to fall in love with the wrong man.

Born in Lindsay, Ontario, Canada, in 1871, Pearl Taylor was described by a childhood friend as "very pretty . . . lithesome, blithe, and witty, gushing with fun and jollity, also a wonderful dancer." But apparently, "She was too amorous, accepted too many dates with handsome young men, which finally caused her undoing."

Pearl attended boarding school, and at age sixteen, she eloped with a handsome, smooth-talking gambler and sometimes bartender, probably named Frank Hart. The young couple seemed happy enough at first, but when Hart's earnings took a turn for the worse, which they often did, so did his temper.

Through the years Pearl left her abusive husband on numerous occasions, but she would always return when he plaintively apologized for his violent behavior. She couldn't resist his handsome face and beguiling words of endearment.

The couple reunited in 1893 and traveled to Chicago to attend the World's Columbian Exposition. While her husband earned a few dollars as a barker, Pearl visited Buffalo Bill's Wild West Show and became enamored with the excitement and lure of the untamed West. When Hart mistreated her once again, she hopped a train that dropped her off in the coal-mining community of Trinidad, Colorado.

Pearl may have arrived in Colorado on the arms of piano player Dan Bandman. Other reports indicate she arrived alone and worked as a domestic, hotel maid, or cook. Then there are those who insist she had already acquired a fondness for morphine and made her living as a soiled dove in a bawdy house.

Pearl refused to elaborate on these years. In an interview with *Cosmopolitan* magazine in 1899, she said, "I do not care to dwell on this period of my life. It is sufficient to say that I went from one city to another until some time later I arrived in Phoenix." Before leaving Trinidad, she gave birth to a son.

After she reconciled with her husband in 1895, the couple lived in Phoenix, enjoyed wedded bliss for about three years, and had a daughter. After a particularly violent fight that left Pearl unconscious, she again left Hart and went east to work as a domestic. She sent her children to live with her mother.

Hart persuaded Pearl to return to him once more and the couple spent some time in Tucson before he supposedly left to fight in the Spanish-American War. Relocating to Phoenix, Pearl declared she hoped the Spanish would "get him."

She moved into a tent on the banks of the Gila River and cooked for miners in the Mammoth area. When her health deteriorated, Joe Boot, a sometimes miner who had befriended the struggling woman, suggested the two of them try their luck around Globe, a seemingly more profitable mining district. She found work as a cook in a Globe boardinghouse until one of the larger quarries closed and she was again destitute.

About this time Pearl received a letter from her brother claiming he was in a scrape and needed money. She sent him what she could, but shortly, another letter arrived saying her mother, who now lived in Ohio, was dying and wanted to see her daughter one last time. With no funds Pearl was frantic to get to the woman who had never given up on her wayward daughter, the woman who watched over her children.

Although Pearl said in her *Cosmopolitan* interview that Joe "proposed that we rob the Globe stage," she later left a note saying she "forced Joe Boot at the point of my gun to help me hold up the stage. It was my fault, not his. He loved me and did as I said. If he had not, I sure would have killed him and he knew it too." She went on to say she would have done anything to get to her dying mother—including robbing a stage.

As Joe and Pearl fled after the robbery, they planned to head for Benson, hop a train and travel whichever way the rails were running. Instead they entered Benson as prisoners of Sheriff Truman. He transported them by rail to Casa Grande, then by buckboard to the Florence jail, arriving with his passengers on June 4.

After Pearl tried to fake her suicide by throwing talcum powder in her face, Truman decided his facility was not suitable for female occupants. He bought Pearl a proper dress and hat to take the place of her masculine attire and escorted her to the Tucson jail to await trial.

But Pearl had no intention of waiting for the courts to decide her fate. She was on a mission to see her "darling old gray haired mother." On October 12, 1899, after luring a love-struck, incarcerated bicycle thief named Edward Hogan (or Ed Sherwood) into her plan of escape, Pearl wiggled out of a hole her paramour had cut in her makeshift cell and escaped into the night.

In the note she left behind in the Tucson jail confessing it was her idea to rob the stagecoach, she also warned, "If she [her mother] has died since my arrest God pity those who kept me from her. I shall have no pity and shall devote my entire life to killing all who detained me."

The fugitives clung between two rail cars on the eastbound train out of Tucson headed for Lordsburg, New Mexico, where they parted ways. By the time Pearl reached Deming, her whereabouts were well known to U.S. Marshal George A. Scarborough, who kept her under surveillance until Hogan/Sherwood reappeared. After arresting the pair, he notified Tucson authorities to come and get their wandering fugitives.

As she boarded the train in Deming for the return trip to Tucson, Pearl regaled the crowd that came to see her with capricious stories about her famed stagecoach heist. Thus the elaborate saga of her days as a lady bandit began to multiply and merge fact with fiction.

Pearl's trial commenced in Florence in November 1899, before the Honorable Fletcher M. Doan. She batted her eyes at the jurors and shed a few tears while relating the sad tale of her dying mother. Purportedly, she even evoked the suffrage movement into her pathetic pleas, claiming she would never "consent to be tried under a law which my sex had no voice in making." And it worked. Ten minutes after the jurors received the case, they returned a verdict of not guilty for the darling Pearl of the West.

Furious with her acquittal, Judge Doan immediately had her rearrested and charged with stealing the stage driver's pistol. A new jury quickly found her guilty, and Doan sentenced her to five years in Yuma Territorial Prison, proclaiming it would take at least that long to alleviate her proclivity for robbing stagecoaches.

As the train carrying Pearl to prison passed through the small communities that lined the rails from Florence to Yuma, the *Coconino Sun* noted she could be seen "with a big cigar in her mouth rivaling the efforts of the locomotive to charge the atmosphere with smoke."

In the meantime Joe Boot was tried separately, found guilty of robbing the stagecoach, and sentenced to serve thirty years in Yuma

Territorial Prison. Boot became a model prisoner. He was made a trustee and allowed to drive food wagons to work crews outside the prison walls. On February 6, 1901, he drove through the prison gates as usual and never looked back. He was never seen again.

Yuma Territorial Prison was home to several women before Pearl Hart, but she was certainly the most famous female inmate. Construction on the adobe and stone penitentiary began in 1875, and work continued on the edifice the entire thirty-three years of the prison's existence. Yuma citizens called the modern facility "the Country Club on the Colorado," protesting that prisoners basked in the luxurious setting along the banks of the Colorado River. Pearl might have disagreed with them as she languished in her caliche cell where temperatures often registered well over 100 degrees.

In the spring of 1901, Pearl's sister, Mrs. C.P. Frizzell, visited her in Yuma. Mrs. Frizzell claimed she had written a play, *The Arizona Bandit*, detailing her sister's adventures and expected Pearl to star in the presentation after her release. However, no proof exists that the play was every performed.

In the fall of 1902, the female section of the prison was becoming exceedingly full as more women were invited to spend time in the Yuma facility. To alleviate the overcrowding, the prison superintendent recommended the release of Pearl Hart, along with seventeen-year-old Rosa Duran, who had served thirteen months of her three-year term for grand larceny. In a November 15 letter to the Board of Control, the superintendent also recommended that Pearl be ordered to "remain out of the Territory of Arizona for the term of her sentence." Two days later, the board approved the release of the two women.

The superintendent received several letters from Pearl's sister promising to pay the fare to Kansas City, Missouri, so Pearl could reunite with her family. She departed Arizona on December 15, 1902.

But another scenario involving Pearl's release is much more damning to those entrusted with her care. In September 1956 journalist Bert Fireman reported in the *Arizona Republic* magazine that Pearl was pregnant when she was released from prison. According to Fireman, in 1954, after all individuals involved in the cover-up had died, George Smalley, secretary to Governor Alexander O. Brodie in 1902, claimed the prison superintendent had told Brodie that, according to the prison doctor, Pearl was pregnant. Supposedly, only three men had access to her cell: the governor, the superintendent, and a trustee. To avoid any scandal she was released with the stipulation she leave Arizona.

No records have materialized confirming that Pearl Hart gave birth after her discharge from prison. In retrospect this account might be looked upon as yet another trick up Pearl's conniving sleeve to obtain an early release.

A few months later, while selling cigars in Kansas City, Pearl was arrested for "complicity with thieves." At the time she was using the name Mrs. L.P. Keele. After that Pearl Hart disappeared from public view, at least for a while.

Sightings of Pearl continued to pop up as the years rolled along. In 1928 she may have returned to Tucson. Several people claimed they saw her hanging around the courthouse jail where she was once held on charges of robbing the Globe stage. She would have been about fifty-seven years old.

More substantial evidence that Pearl returned to Arizona lies in the history of Globe, Arizona, as told by Clara T. Woody in 1977. Woody served as census taker for Globe during the 1940s and claimed she met Pearl on several occasions. She said Pearl married rancher Calvin Bywater and lived quietly on the Dripping Springs Ranch, not far from Cane Springs Canyon, the scene of that long-ago stage robbery. If this was the notorious Pearl Hart, she never admitted her past. Until her death on December 30, 1955, Mrs. Calvin Bywater never used her first name, nor did she give any indication she had lived an outlaw life.

Neither pistol nor pen gave Pearl Hart a life of respectability. Wherever she lies today, she will always be remembered as Arizona Territory's bandit queen, a woman of fact and fiction, fame and fascination, who was both adored and vilified.

Bibliography

Barnes, Will C. *Arizona Place Names*. Tucson: University of Arizona Press, 1988.

Erwin, Allen A. *The Southwest of John H. Slaughter, 1841–1922*. Spokane, Wash.: The Arthur H. Clark Company, 1965.

Genung, Dan B. *Death in His Saddlebags: Charles Baldwin Genung, Arizona Pioneer*. Manhattan, Kans: Sunflower University Press, 1992.

Prassel, Frank Richard. *The Great American Outlaw: A Legacy of Fact and Fiction*. Norman, Okla: University of Oklahoma Press, 1993.

Rasch, Philip J. *Desperadoes of Arizona Territory*. Laramie, Wyo.: National Association for Outlaw and Lawman History, Inc. In affiliation with the University of Wyoming, 1999.

Sheridan, Thomas E. *Arizona: A History*. Tucson: University of Arizona Press, 1995.

Sonnichsen, C. L. *Billy King's Tombstone: The Private Life of an Arizona Boom Town*. Tucson: University of Arizona Press, 1972.

Wagoner, Jay J. *Arizona Territory 1863–1912: A Political History*. Tucson: University of Arizona Press, 1970.

The Wickenburg Massacre

Barney, James M. "The Wickenburg Massacre." *The Sheriff* 5 no. 3 (October 1946): 15–22.

Farish, Thomas Edwin. *History of Arizona*. Phoenix: State of Arizona, 1918.

Hawkins, Helen B. *A History of Wickenburg to 1875*. Wickenburg: Maricopa County Historical Society, 1971. Thesis, Arizona State College, 1950.

Miller, Joseph, ed. *The Arizona Story*. New York: Hastings House, 1952.

Smith, Bill W., comp. *A Collection of Newspaper Articles, Letters, and Reports Regarding the Wickenburg Massacre and Subsequent Camp Date Creek Incident*. Phoenix: Bill W. Smith, 1989.

Truman, Ben C. *Occidental Sketches*. San Francisco: San Francisco News Company, 1881.

Wilson, R. Michael. *Drenched in Blood, Rigid in Death: The True Story of the Wickenburg Massacre*. Las Vegas: Juniper Twig Books, 2000.

Frank Nashville "Buckskin Frank" Leslie

Bailey, Lynn R. and Don Chaput. *Cochise County Stalwarts: A Who's Who of the Territorial Years*. Vols. 1 and 2. Tucson: Westernlore Press, 2000.

Breakenridge, William M. *Helldorado: Bringing the Law to the Mesquite*. Lincoln, Nebr.: University of Nebraska Press, 1992. Originally published 1928.

Chafin, Carl, ed. *The Private Journals of George Whitwell Parsons*. Vol. 2. Tombstone, Ariz.: Cochise Classics, 1997.

Chaput, Don. *"Buckskin Frank" Leslie*. Tucson: Westernlore Press, 1999.

Martin, Douglas D. *Silver, Sex and Six Guns: Tombstone Saga of the Life of Buckskin Frank Leslie*. Tombstone, Ariz.: Tombstone Epitaph, 1962.

Rickards, Colin. *"Buckskin Frank" Leslie: Gunman of Tombstone.* El Paso, Texas: Texas Western College Press, 1964.

Traywick, Ben T. *The Chronicles of Tombstone.* Tombstone, Ariz.: Red Marie's Bookstore, 1986.

The Grime/Hawley Heist

Bigando, Robert. *Globe, Arizona: The Life and Times of a Western Mining Town, 1864–1917.* Globe, Ariz.: American Globe Publishing Company, 1989.

Hayes, Jess G. *Boots and Bullets: The Life and Times of John W. Wentworth.* Tucson: University of Arizona Press, 1967.

Heiter, Paul T. "Popular Justice Run Amok: The Globe Lynchings of 1882." Yuma, Ariz.: Paper presented at Arizona Historical Society Convention, 1999.

Walters, Lorenzo D. Tombstone's Yesterday manuscript collection, 1928–1928. Tucson, Ariz.: Arizona Historical Society.

———. *Tombstone's Yesterday.* Glorieta, N.Mex.: The Rio Grande Press, Inc., 1968. First published 1928.

Wilson, R. Michael. *Crime & Punishment in Early Arizona.* Las Vegas: Stagecoach Books, 2004.

Woody, Clara T. and Milton L. Schwartz. *Globe, Arizona.* Tucson: The Arizona Historical Society, 1977.

James Addison Reavis

Burgess, Glenn, ed. *Mount Graham Profiles: Volume 2, Ryder Ridgeway Collection*. Safford, Ariz.: Graham County Historical Society, 1988.

Cookridge, E. H. *The Baron of Arizona*. New York: Ballantine Books, 1967.

Farrell, Robert J., ed. *They Left Their Mark*. Phoenix: Arizona Department of Transportation, 1997.

Powell, Donald M. "The 'Baron of Arizona' Self Revealed: A Letter to His Lawyer in 1894." *Arizona and the West* 1, no. 2 (summer 1959): 161–73.

———. *The Peralta Grant: James Addison Reavis and the Barony of Arizona*. Norman, Okla.: University of Oklahoma Press, 1960.

Tipton, Will M. "The Prince of Imposters." *Land of Sunshine* 8, nos. 3 & 4 (February and March 1898): 106–18, 161–70.

Charles P. Stanton

Barkdull, Tom. *Lonesome Walls: An Odyssey Through Ghost Towns of the Old West*. New York: Exposition Press, 1971.

Crombie, M. Katherine, Chris T. Gholson, Dante S. Lauretta, and Erik B. Melchiorre. *Rich Hill: The History of Arizona's Most Amazing Gold District*. Tucson: Golden Retriever Publications, 2002.

Esenwein, William. *The Private Empire of Charlie P. Stanton, King of Con Men*. Stanton, Ariz.: Esenwein, 1973.

Genung, Charles Baldwin, comp. *Yavapai Country Memories, 1863–1894*. nos. 43 & 44 (spring & fall 1982): 66–69.

Gould, P. B. *The Irish Lord: Charles B. Stanton.* Congress, Ariz.: PBG Press, 2005.

Lauer, Charles D. *Tales of Arizona Territory.* Phoenix: Golden West Publishers, 1990.

Stano, Mary G. "Charles Stanton: He Ruled a Town by Betrayal and Murder." *The Nevadan Today.* March 26, 1989.

The Apache Kid

Forrest, Earle R. and Edwin B. Hill. *Lone War Trail of Apache Kid.* Pasadena, Calif.: Trail's End Publishing Co., Inc., 1947.

Freeman, Dr. M. P. *The Dread Apache: That Early-Day Scourge of the Southwest.* Tucson: n.p., 1915.

de la Garza, Phyllis. *The Apache Kid.* Tucson: Westernlore Press, 1995.

Genung, Dan B. Genung Reminscences manuscript collection. Tucson: Arizona Historical Society.

Genung Jr., Dan B. "The Death of the Apache Kid." *Arizona Highways Magazine.* November 1995: 32–35.

Pool, Frank M. "The Apache Kid." *The Sheriff* 6, no. 2 (March 1947): 18–24.

Ringgold, Jennie Parks. *Frontier Days in the Southwest: Pioneer Days in Old Arizona.* San Antonio, Texas: The Naylor Company, 1952.

Robinson, Sherry. *Apache Voices: Their Stories of Survival As Told to Eve Ball.* Albuquerque: University of New Mexico Press, 2000.

Sparks, William. *The Apache Kid, a Bear Fight and Other True Stories of the Old West.* Los Angeles: Skelton Publishing Company, 1926.

Wharfield, H. B. "Footnotes to History: Apache Kid and the Record." *The Journal of Arizona History* 6, no. 1 (spring 1965): 37–46.

Williamson, Dan R. "The Apache Kid: Renegade of the West." *Arizona Highways Magazine* 15, no. 5 (May 1939): 14–17.

Wham Paymaster Robbery

Ball, Larry D. *Ambush at Bloody Run: The Wham Paymaster Robbery of 1889.* Tucson: The Arizona Historical Society, 2000.

——. *The United States Marshals of New Mexico and Arizona Territories, 1846–1912.* Albuquerque: University of New Mexico Press, 1978.

Block, Eugene B. *Great Stagecoach Robbers of the West.* New York: Doubleday & Company, Inc., 1962.

Marshall, Otto Miller. *The Wham Paymaster Robbery, Boldest in Arizona History, May 11, 1889.* Sponsored and distributed by the Pima Chamber of Commerce, April 1967.

Schubert, Frank N. *Black Valor: Buffalo Soldiers and the Medal of Honor, 1870–1898.* Wilmington, Del.: Scholarly Resources, Inc., 1997.

——. *Voices of the Buffalo Soldier: Records, Reports, and Recollections of Military Life and Service in the West.* Albuquerque: University of New Mexico Press, 2003.

Upton, Larry T. and Larry D. Ball. "Who Robbed Major Wham? Facts and Folklore Behind Arizona's Great Paymaster Robbery." *Journal of Arizona History* 38, no. 2 (summer 1997): 99–134.

Augustine Chacón

Edwards, Harold L. "This is the Greatest Day of My Life: The Hanging of Augustin Chacón." *True West*. November 1995: 14–21.

Burgess, Glenn, ed. *Mount Graham Profiles, Volume 2, Ryder Ridgeway Collection*. Safford, Ariz.: Graham County Historical Society, 1988.

Rickards, Colin. "The Hairy One—Arizona's Deadly Bandit." *The West: True Stories of the Old West* 14, no. 1 (December 1970): 30–31, 56–64.

James Fleming Parker

Allen, Paul L. and Peter M. Pegnam. *Arizona Territory: Baptism in Blood*. Tucson: Tucson Citizen Publishing Company, 1990.

Miller, Joseph, ed. *The Arizona Story*. New York: Hastings House, 1952.

Trimble, Marshall. *Arizona: A Cavalcade of History*. Tucson: Treasure Chest Publications, 1989.

———. *Arizona Highways: The Law of the Gun*. Phoenix: Arizona Department of Transportation, State of Arizona, 1997.

Way, Thomas E. *The Parker Story*. Prescott, Ariz.: Prescott Graphics, 1981.

Weiner, Melissa Ruffner. *Prescott Yesteryears: Life in Arizona's First Territorial Capital*. Prescott, Ariz.: Primrose Press, 1979.

Wilson, R. Michael. *Crime & Punishment in Early Arizona*. Las Vegas: Stagecoach Books, 2004.

Albert Wright "Burt" Alvord

Block, Eugene B. *Great Train Robberies of the West.* New York: Coward-McCann, Inc., 1959.

Bond, Ervin. *Percy Bowden: Born to be a Frontier Lawman.* Douglas, Ariz.: Bond, 1976.

Chaput, Don. *The Odyssey of Burt Alvord: Lawman, Train Robber, Fugitive.* Tucson: Westernlore Press, 2000.

Coolidge, Dane. *Fighting Men of the West.* New York: E.P. Dutton & Co., Inc., 1932.

Haley, J. Evetts. *Jeff Milton: A Good Man with a Gun.* Norman, Okla.: University of Oklahoma Press, 1948.

Hendricks, George D. *The Bad Man of the West.* San Antonio, Texas: The Naylor Company, 1942.

Patterson, Richard. *The Train Robbery Era: An Encyclopedic History.* Boulder, Colo.: Pruett Publishing Company, 1991.

Ringgold, Jennie Parks. *Frontier Days in the Southwest.* San Antonio, Texas: The Naylor Company, 1952.

Theobald, John and Lillian. *Wells, Fargo in Arizona Territory.* Tempe, Ariz.: Arizona Historical Foundation, 1978.

White, Scott, as told to John Edwin Hogg. "Bad Men's Nemesis: The adventures and experiences of an Arizona sheriff, in a land and a time when a man often wore a moustache, but always wore a gun." *Touring Topics,* April 1931: 25–26.

Pearl Hart

Aikman, Duncan. *Calamity Jane and the Lady Wildcats.* New York: Henry Holt and Company, 1927.

Allen, Paul L. and Peter M. Pegnam. *Arizona Territory: Baptism in Blood.* Tucson: Tucson Citizen Publishing Company, 1990.

Armitage, Shelley. "Pearl Hart: Desperate Woman or Desperado?" In *With Badges and Bullets: Lawmen & Outlaws in the Old West.* Richard W. Etulain & Glenda Riley, eds. Golden, Colo.: Fulcrum Publishing, 1999.

Brent, William and Milarde Brent. *The Hell Hole.* Yuma, Ariz.: William Brent and Milarde Brent, 1962.

Brown, Wynne. *More than Petticoats: Remarkable Arizona Women.* Guilford, Conn.: The Globe Pequot Press, 2003.

Hart, Pearl. "An Arizona Episode." *Cosmopolitan* 27, no. 6 (October 1899), 673–77.

Horan, James D. *Desperate Women.* New York: G.P. Putnam's Sons, 1952.

Klungness, Elizabeth J., *Prisoners in Petticoats: The Yuma Territorial Prison and Its Women.* Yuma, Ariz.: Yuma County Historical Society Publications, 1993.

Walters, Lorenzo D. Tombstone's Yesterday manuscript collection, 1928-1928. Tucson: Arizona Historical Society.

———. *Tombstone's Yesterday.* Glorieta, N.Mex.: The Rio Grande Press, Inc., 1968. First published 1928.

Bibliography

Wilson, R. Michael. *Encyclopedia of Stagecoach Robbery in Arizona.* Las Vegas: RaMA Press, 2003.

Woody, Clara T. and Milton L. Schwartz. *Globe, Arizona.* Tucson: The Arizona Historical Society, 1977.

About the Author

J an Cleere writes extensively about the desert Southwest, its unique characters, creatures, and vegetation. Her articles have appeared in regional and national publications. When not writing about long-forgotten pioneers, strange-looking cacti, or sharp-snouted javelina, she can usually be found perched in front of a cobweb-encrusted tome searching for that elusive piece of information that lends credence or refutation to an often-repeated but unproven antiquated yarn. Jan is also the author of *More than Petticoats: Remarkable Nevada Women* (The Globe Pequot Press, 2005). She resides under the shadows of the Catalina Mountains in Tucson, Arizona, with her husband and a myriad of wild critters that visit her desert home.

WOMEN
of the
WILD WEST

From entertainer to soldier, doctor to rancher, read about the lives of the exceptional women who pioneered the American West.

- Biographies
- Diaries and letters
- Memoirs
- Regional history
- Westward travel narratives